Military instructions for the cavallrie, or, Rules and directions for the service of horse collected out of divers forrein authours, ancient and modern, and rectified and supplied according to the present practice of the Low-Countrey warres. (1644)

John Cruso

Military instructions for the cavallrie, or, Rules and directions for the service of horse collected out of divers forrein authours, ancient and modern, and rectified and supplied according to the present practice of the Low-Countrey warres.

Cruso, John, d. 1681.
p. 11-14 wanting.
[9], 51 p., [6] leaves of plates (4 folded) :
Cambridge : Printed by Roger Daniel, 1644.
Wing / C7433
English
Reproduction of the original in the Cambridge University Library

Early English Books Online (EEBO) Editions

Imagine holding history in your hands.

Now you can. Digitally preserved and previously accessible only through libraries as Early English Books Online, this rare material is now available in single print editions. Thousands of books written between 1475 and 1700 and ranging from religion to astronomy, medicine to music, can be delivered to your doorstep in individual volumes of high-quality historical reproductions.

We have been compiling these historic treasures for more than 70 years. Long before such a thing as "digital" even existed, ProQuest founder Eugene Power began the noble task of preserving the British Museum's collection on microfilm. He then sought out other rare and endangered titles, providing unparalleled access to these works and collaborating with the world's top academic institutions to make them widely available for the first time. This project furthers that original vision.

These texts have now made the full journey -- from their original printing-press versions available only in rare-book rooms to online library access to new single volumes made possible by the partnership between artifact preservation and modern printing technology. A portion of the proceeds from every book sold supports the libraries and institutions that made this collection possible, and that still work to preserve these invaluable treasures passed down through time.

This is history, traveling through time since the dawn of printing to your own personal library.

Initial Proquest EEBO Print Editions collections include:

Early Literature

This comprehensive collection begins with the famous Elizabethan Era that saw such literary giants as Chaucer, Shakespeare and Marlowe, as well as the introduction of the sonnet. Traveling through Jacobean and Restoration literature, the highlight of this series is the Pollard and Redgrave 1475-1640 selection of the rarest works from the English Renaissance.

Early Documents of World History

This collection combines early English perspectives on world history with documentation of Parliament records, royal decrees and military documents that reveal the delicate balance of Church and State in early English government. For social historians, almanacs and calendars offer insight into daily life of common citizens. This exhaustively complete series presents a thorough picture of history through the English Civil War.

Historical Almanacs

Historically, almanacs served a variety of purposes from the more practical, such as planting and harvesting crops and plotting nautical routes, to predicting the future through the movements of the stars. This collection provides a wide range of consecutive years of "almanacks" and calendars that depict a vast array of everyday life as it was several hundred years ago.

Early History of Astronomy & Space

Humankind has studied the skies for centuries, seeking to find our place in the universe. Some of the most important discoveries in the field of astronomy were made in these texts recorded by ancient stargazers, but almost as impactful were the perspectives of those who considered their discoveries to be heresy. Any independent astronomer will find this an invaluable collection of titles arguing the truth of the cosmic system.

Early History of Industry & Science

Acting as a kind of historical Wall Street, this collection of industry manuals and records explores the thriving industries of construction; textile, especially wool and linen; salt; livestock; and many more.

Early English Wit, Poetry & Satire

The power of literary device was never more in its prime than during this period of history, where a wide array of political and religious satire mocked the status quo and poetry called humankind to transcend the rigors of daily life through love, God or principle. This series comments on historical patterns of the human condition that are still visible today.

Early English Drama & Theatre

This collection needs no introduction, combining the works of some of the greatest canonical writers of all time, including many plays composed for royalty such as Queen Elizabeth I and King Edward VI. In addition, this series includes history and criticism of drama, as well as examinations of technique.

Early History of Travel & Geography

Offering a fascinating view into the perception of the world during the sixteenth and seventeenth centuries, this collection includes accounts of Columbus's discovery of the Americas and encompasses most of the Age of Discovery, during which Europeans and their descendants intensively explored and mapped the world. This series is a wealth of information from some the most groundbreaking explorers.

Early Fables & Fairy Tales

This series includes many translations, some illustrated, of some of the most well-known mythologies of today, including Aesop's Fables and English fairy tales, as well as many Greek, Latin and even Oriental parables and criticism and interpretation on the subject.

Early Documents of Language & Linguistics

The evolution of English and foreign languages is documented in these original texts studying and recording early philology from the study of a variety of languages including Greek, Latin and Chinese, as well as multilingual volumes, to current slang and obscure words. Translations from Latin, Hebrew and Aramaic, grammar treatises and even dictionaries and guides to translation make this collection rich in cultures from around the world.

Early History of the Law

With extensive collections of land tenure and business law "forms" in Great Britain, this is a comprehensive resource for all kinds of early English legal precedents from feudal to constitutional law, Jewish and Jesuit law, laws about public finance to food supply and forestry, and even "immoral conditions." An abundance of law dictionaries, philosophy and history and criticism completes this series.

Early History of Kings, Queens and Royalty

This collection includes debates on the divine right of kings, royal statutes and proclamations, and political ballads and songs as related to a number of English kings and queens, with notable concentrations on foreign rulers King Louis IX and King Louis XIV of France, and King Philip II of Spain. Writings on ancient rulers and royal tradition focus on Scottish and Roman kings, Cleopatra and the Biblical kings Nebuchadnezzar and Solomon.

Early History of Love, Marriage & Sex

Human relationships intrigued and baffled thinkers and writers well before the postmodern age of psychology and self-help. Now readers can access the insights and intricacies of Anglo-Saxon interactions in sex and love, marriage and politics, and the truth that lies somewhere in between action and thought.

Early History of Medicine, Health & Disease

This series includes fascinating studies on the human brain from as early as the 16th century, as well as early studies on the physiological effects of tobacco use. Anatomy texts, medical treatises and wound treatment are also discussed, revealing the exponential development of medical theory and practice over more than two hundred years.

Early History of Logic, Science and Math

The "hard sciences" developed exponentially during the 16th and 17th centuries, both relying upon centuries of tradition and adding to the foundation of modern application, as is evidenced by this extensive collection. This is a rich collection of practical mathematics as applied to business, carpentry and geography as well as explorations of mathematical instruments and arithmetic; logic and logicians such as Aristotle and Socrates; and a number of scientific disciplines from natural history to physics.

Early History of Military, War and Weaponry

Any professional or amateur student of war will thrill at the untold riches in this collection of war theory and practice in the early Western World. The Age of Discovery and Enlightenment was also a time of great political and religious unrest, revealed in accounts of conflicts such as the Wars of the Roses.

Early History of Food

This collection combines the commercial aspects of food handling, preservation and supply to the more specific aspects of canning and preserving, meat carving, brewing beer and even candy-making with fruits and flowers, with a large resource of cookery and recipe books. Not to be forgotten is a "the great eater of Kent," a study in food habits.

Early History of Religion

From the beginning of recorded history we have looked to the heavens for inspiration and guidance. In these early religious documents, sermons, and pamphlets, we see the spiritual impact on the lives of both royalty and the commoner. We also get insights into a clergy that was growing ever more powerful as a political force. This is one of the world's largest collections of religious works of this type, revealing much about our interpretation of the modern church and spirituality.

Early Social Customs

Social customs, human interaction and leisure are the driving force of any culture. These unique and quirky works give us a glimpse of interesting aspects of day-to-day life as it existed in an earlier time. With books on games, sports, traditions, festivals, and hobbies it is one of the most fascinating collections in the series.

The BiblioLife Network

This project was made possible in part by the BiblioLife Network (BLN), a project aimed at addressing some of the huge challenges facing book preservationists around the world. The BLN includes libraries, library networks, archives, subject matter experts, online communities and library service providers. We believe every book ever published should be available as a high-quality print reproduction; printed on-demand anywhere in the world. This insures the ongoing accessibility of the content and helps generate sustainable revenue for the libraries and organizations that work to preserve these important materials.

The following book is in the "public domain" and represents an authentic reproduction of the text as printed by the original publisher. While we have attempted to accurately maintain the integrity of the original work, there are sometimes problems with the original work or the micro-film from which the books were digitized. This can result in minor errors in reproduction. Possible imperfections include missing and blurred pages, poor pictures, markings and other reproduction issues beyond our control. Because this work is culturally important, we have made it available as part of our commitment to protecting, preserving, and promoting the world's literature.

GUIDE TO FOLD-OUTS MAPS and OVERSIZED IMAGES

The book you are reading was digitized from microfilm captured over the past thirty to forty years. Years after the creation of the original microfilm, the book was converted to digital files and made available in an online database.

In an online database, page images do not need to conform to the size restrictions found in a printed book. When converting these images back into a printed bound book, the page sizes are standardized in ways that maintain the detail of the original. For large images, such as fold-out maps, the original page image is split into two or more pages

Guidelines used to determine how to split the page image follows:

• Some images are split vertically; large images require vertical and horizontal splits.
• For horizontal splits, the content is split left to right.
• For vertical splits, the content is split from top to bottom.
• For both vertical and horizontal splits, the image is processed from top left to bottom right.

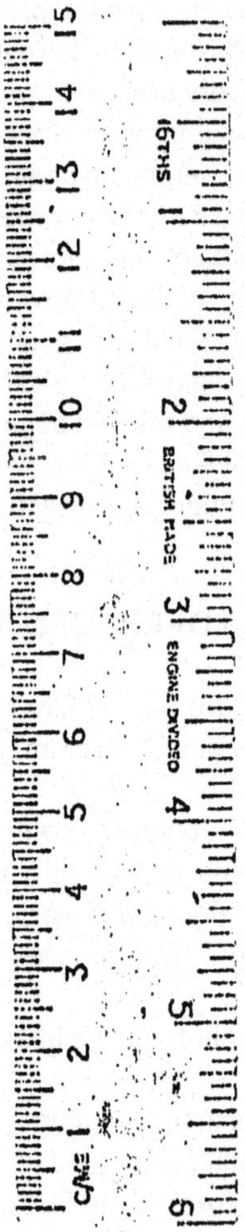

Military Instructions

for the

CAVALLRIE:

Or
RULES AND DIRECTIONS
for the
SERVICE OF HORSE,

Collected out of divers forrein Authours,
Ancient and Modern:

And

Rectified and supplied, according to the present practise
of the Lovv-Country *Warres.*

Prov. 21. 31.
The horse is prepared for battell: but victory is from the Lord.

CAMBRIDGE:
Printed by Roger Daniel, Printer to the
Universitie. 1644.

MILITARIE
INSTRUCTIONS
for the
CAVALL'RIE:
According to the
Moderne warrs.

CAMBRIDGE:
Printed by Roger Daniel printer to the
Universitie. 1644
And are to be sold by W: Hope at the Unicorn in
Cornhill neare the Royall Exchange

Cam. a. b444. 1

Military Instructions
for the
CAVALLRIE:
Or
RULES AND DIRECTIONS
for the
SERVICE OF HORSE,

Collected out of divers forrein Authours,
Ancient and Modern :

And
Rectified and supplied, according to the present practise
of the Lovv-Countrey Warres.

PROV. 21. 31.
The horse is prepared for battell : but victory is from the Lord.

CAMBRIDGE :
Printed by ROGER DANIEL, Printer to the
Universitie.   1 6 4 4.

24

TO
THE RIGHT HONOURABLE
THOMAS,
Earl of *Arundell* and *Surrey*, Earl Marſhall of ENGLAND,
of the moſt Noble Order of the Garter, Knight:
Lord Lieutenant of His Majeſties forces in Norfolk
and Norwich, *and one of His Majeſties moſt*
Honourable Privy-Councell.

Right Honourable;

Aving lately finiſhed this diſcourſe of Cavallry, intending it onely for my private uſe and information, it had the fortune to light into the hands of two noble and judici-ous peruſers. The one (during the ſhort diſcontinuance from his regiment, while it lay in winter garriſon) hath been courteouſly pleaſed to go through it, correcting what here and there was amiſſe, ſupplying ſome things defective, and mani-feſting his approbation of it with an *Imprimatur.* The other (among other things) hath chiefly vouchſafed his aſſiſtance and directions for the managing of the horſe, and handling of arms ; as being a thing princi-pally neceſſary, and that wherein authours have hitherto been defective. Theſe conſiderations, together with the commanding requeſt (among others) of ſome of your Honours Deputy-Lieutenants (not any arrogan-cie or ambition of mine) have prevailed with me (in hope of publick good) to expoſe theſe weak eſſaies to the publick view of the world. Now ſince the patronizing of a work of Marſhall diſcipline, ſeemeth moſt properly to belong to the Earl Marſhall; and that charge wherewith I ſtand entruſted within your Lordſhips Lieutenancy, obligeth me in du-ty to conſecrate the beſt of my endeavours to your Honours ſervice : May it pleaſe your Honour (of your innate clemency, and favour to Arts) to vouchſafe your honourable patronage and protection on theſe poore labours of his, who ſhall ever (in all humility) remain,

Your Honours

dutifully devoted ſervant,

A 3   J. C.

TO THE READER.

OF making many books there is no end, said the wise King many ages past; yet for some Arts and faculties, I suppose (even in this printing age of ours) we may complain of scarcitie. For among so many Authors ancient and modern, which have written of the Art Military, is it not strange that hardly any have fully handled that which concerneth the Cavalry? Among the ancients Ælian hath somewhat touched upon the manner of ordering the horse among the Grecians, and Vegetius (where he speaketh of the Romane Cavalrie) lightly passeth it over, and concludeth in [c] these words, De equitatu sunt multa præcepta: sed cùm hæc pars militiæ usu exercitii, armorum genere, & equorum nobilitate profecerit, ex libris nihil arbitror colligendum, cùm præsens doctrina sufficiat. Now the reason why they (bestowing their chief labour about the Infantery) left so little direction for the horse, may be, either because that (both with Grecians and Romanes) the [b] foot were of greatest esteem (as that wherein their chief strength consisted, and whereon they principally relyed) and so the lesse regard was had of the horse; or else because the service of horse was not [c] grown to that perfection in those times, which it since attained. For what great effect could be expected of horse using no [d] bridle, and having neither [e] saddle nor stirrops: bearing onely [f] a weak slender pole (which the very motion of the horse would shake in pieces) and a little round target (as the Romanes manner was at first) or else a staffe or kind of [g] lance (which they afterward used in imitation of the Grecians) with three or foure darts? and having no surer stay to counterpoise their forced motion, what certainty or violence could they use, either in charging or casting their weapons? and whereas they usually had of the light armed foot [h] intermingled among them, how could they be so serried together for the shock as to do any great effect in making impressions upon their enemies? which surely was the cause they were often commanded [i] to alight, and (forsaking their horses) to fight on foot. But for modern Authors there is not the like reason: and yet of so many as have written, none have treated of rules and instructions for the Cavalry, untill lately George Basta, Count of the holy Empire, and Luys Melzo Knight of Malta, wrote their books of Cavalry. These works of theirs afford good directions: but yet it may be said of them as Ælian saith of those Authors which had written before him, [k] That they had so written, as if none should read them but such as were already skilfull in the Art Military. This defect one Walhausen taketh upon him to supply; something he hath done in the motions. but for the first rudiments, for the handling of arms, &c. he (as all others) is silent. But these and the like being written in the forrein languages, and among so many of our military Pamphlets none treating of Cavalry; I have adventured (though altogether unfit for such a task) to employ some idle houres in the diligent reading, and conferring of the said Authors together with such other books and informations as I could obtain out of the Low-countreys and other places, for my better satisfaction herein: [l] endeavouring to extract the marrow and quintessence of their prolixer discourses, and to digest them into such a method, as I conceived might afford brevity and perspicuity: wherein I have observed to go upon good grounds, affirming nothing of mine [m] own authority. It is true, I have sometimes made bold to dissent from others. but adding my reason, and leaving the judicious Reader to his liberty. For the style, I conceived the [n] bluntest and plainest to be most proper for the subject. If my annotations be displeasing to any, they may use them like Countrey stiles, and step over them. To others they may serve to shew the truth of that assertion, That a [o] meer practicall knowledge cannot make a perfect souldier: for had we not been beholding to [p] books. the Military Art (in all likelihood) had been utterly obscured from our knowledge. For what is there in these modern warres, which is not borrowed from antiquity? wherein we follow them step by step (mutatis mutandis, the later inventions of fire-weapons, and the use and dependancy thereof onely excepted) not onely in the manner, but even retaining their very words of command, as in this Treatise is partly shewed, and would be more manifestly apparent if the subject were Infanterie; which no way disparageth the modern practise, but rather (for the antiquity of it) gives it the more respect and estimation.

Eccles. 12. 12:
a Lib. 3. c. 26.
b Multi reipub. suæ necessarii pedes, equitesque vixisse.
Veg. lib 2. cap. 1.
c Equitatu Romanorum militum minus satis est, unde nostri jam potius exilisio nati est. Scipio Ammiratus, Differt. polit. lib. 19.
d When they were to charge the enemy, they used to pull off their bridles. T. Liu. lib. 4.
e Liu. at Polyb. lib. 3. 219. 210.
f Polyb. lib. 6.
g Comm.
h Cæs. Com. lib. 1. cap. 17. So did the Germanes, of whose light armed foot Cæsar reporteth thus, Tanta erat horum ex usu jam celeritas, ut jubig eoum sub. levatis, cursum adæquarent. Com. 10
i So did the Consul Valerius in the warre against the Sabine. Liu. l. 3. And S Tempanius against the Vessett. Id m lib. 4. and many others.
k Omnia feci et ut minime sensissem, quasi tacere voiunt nos velim nos in nuos, sed sæ in estium vicum paroi, qui explicare filuerunt. Ælian. de instructend. ac exceptis.
l Lapides & ligna ab alio accipio, ædifici tamen extructæ forma nostra. Nec aranearum sane textis idio melior, quis se his atqunt. inc nostri valior, itt ex alienu libamus, ut apes. Lipf. Polit. m Nihil mihi sumo in suis toruntia rebus, sed horum quos supr. renul, et qua ahorus sunt, velut in ordinem epicomia conscribo. Veg l. 1. cap. 28. n Non curantur aliquam verborum ornamenta.
o Proved at large by S. Cl. Edmunds in his preface to Cæsars Commentaries by him translated.
p Apud veteres res militaris in oblivionem sæpius venit, sed à libris repetita est, postea cùm autoritate firmata. Veg. lib. 3 cap. 10.

conquirentes, sed verbis minùs communicatis plenissimè usi, militarem dicendi formam potissimùm secuti sumus. Leo Tact. in Epilog.

Now,

Now, left the Tyro or untutored horseman should be deterred; and should judge his task to be over-great; I have set down a table of the Chapters, that so he may apply himself, onely to those things (at first) which are principally necessary for him to know and practise.

The defects of our trained bands of horse, will argue the work neither unnecessary nor unseasonable, had it but had the hap to light into the hands of a better workman. But as I have seen when an excellent Musician could not be intreated to handle an instrument, some bungler hath fallen upon it; which caused the Musician (out of impatience and indignation) to undertake it; so, if these Essaies may be a means to incite some one or other, better able, q to put pen to paper, I shall think my pains abundantly rewarded. In the mean time I desire they may be received with the right hand, as they are offered; and conclude in the words of the Poet,

—— r Si quid novisti rectius istis,
Candidus imperti; si non, his utere mecum.

q Nam cùm hoc opus, usus potiùs aliorum, quàm mea commendationis causâ aggressus sum, adjuvari me ab his, qui aliquid illi astruunt, non argui erudam. Frontin. in Præf.
r Hor. epist. 6.l.1.

¶ A Table of the Chapters.

An Appendix.

Curteous Reader, this second Edition of my book of *Cavallrie* coming forth without my knowledge, I was disappointed of my purpose of inserting some alterations and additions in their due places: notwithstanding (to satisfie the commanding requests of some Friends) I shall give a touch of some sudden observations, which you may please to referre to their severall Chapters.

Part. 1. Chap. 2. Experience having taught later times that the allowing of Bidets (or Nagges) to the Horsemen, caused a great expense of forrage, and a needlesse consumption of victuall, and great disorders by reason of their boyes; they are not now allowed any naggs, neither in the Armie of the States of the united Provinces, nor in divers other places.

And touching the Captains libertie to choose their own Officers, that is also altered: for the Generall now gives Commissions to the Lieutenant and Cornet as well as to the Captain; yet (in way of favour) the Generall doth oftentimes admit of such Officers as are nominated and presented to him by the Captain.

Chap. 17. We being now fallen into times of Action, and the knowledge of the pay allowed to every Officer and Souldier being so generally necessary, I have thought fit to communicate an Establishment, being that which is at present used: And though I intended onely to speak of so much as concerneth the Horse; yet being of great concernment for the Foot and Train of Artillerie, I shall make bold to digresse a little, and give you a brief and summarie list of all, as followeth.

Officers generall of the Field.

	lib.	sol.	den.
Lord Generall	10. per diem		
Serjeant Major Generall	2		
President of the Councel of Warre		15	
Quartermaster Generall	1		
Provost Marshall Generall		6	8
20. horses allowed him (each 2s 6d)	2	10	
Waggonmaster Generall		10	
two horses allowed him (each 2s 6d)		5	

Officers Generall of the Train.

	lib.	sol.	den.
Treasurer	2		
Mustermaster Generall		15	
three deputies each		5	
Advocate of the Armie	1		
Two Chaplains (each 8s)		16	
One Physician for the L. Generalls person		6	8
One for the Armie		6	8
One Apothecarie		10	
One Chirurgeon		4	
two mates each		2	6
Captain of the Guard	1		
30. men, each		1	6
Commissarie Generall for provision of victuall for the foot		16	
Foure men with horses, each		2	6

The pay of a Regiment of Foot.

	lib.	sol.	den.
Colonell (as Colonell)	1	10	
Lieut. Colonell (as Lieut. Colonell)		15	
Sergeant Major (as Major)		9	
Quartermaster		5	
Provost Marshall		5	
Carriagemaster		3	
Preacher		8	
Chirurgeon		4	
two Mates (2s 6d each)		5	
Captain		15	
Lieutenant		4	
Ensigne		3	
Three Serjeants, each		1	6
One Drum Major		1	6

	lib.	sol.	den.
Two Drums, each		1	
Three Corporalls, each		1	
Souldiers, each			8

The pay of Horse-officers of the Field.

	lib.	sol.	den.
Generall	5		
Lieutenant Generall	2		
Serjeant Major Generall	1	10	
Quartermaster Generall		10	
Two horses Carbines (each 2s 6d)		5	
Commissarie of the provision		16	
Foure horses and men (each 2s 6d)		10	
Provost Marshall		5	
Eight horses, Carbines (each 2s 6d)	1		
Mustermaster Generall		15	
two Deputies, each		5	
Preacher		8	
Chirurgeon		4	
two mates (each 2s 6d)		5	

A Regiment of Cuirassiers.

	lib.	sol.	den.
Colonell (as Colonell)	1	10	
Serjeant Major (as Major)		12	
Captaine	1	4	
six horses (each 3s 6d)	1	1	
Captain-Lieutenant (besides 4. horses)		14	
Lieutenant		8	
foure horses (each 3s 6d)		14	
Cornet (the Generalls 7s,) the rest		6	
three horses (each 3s 6d)		10	6
Quartermaster		4	
two horses (each 3s 6d)		7	
Three Corporalls, each		3	
two horses apiece (each 3s 6d)	1	1	
Two trumpeters, each		3	
A Farrier		3	6
A Sadler		3	6
Carriagemaster		3	6
Preacher		8	
Chirurgeon		4	
Two mates, each		2	6

A 5   Preacher.

	lib.	sol.	den.
Preachers man		2	6
Provost		5	6
Souldiers Chiraffiers, each		3	6

Harquebusiers.

	lib.	sol.	den.
Captain	1	4	
6 Horses, each		2	6
		8	
Lieutenant		2	6
4 horses, each		6	
Cornet		2	6
3 horses, each		4	
Quartermaster		2	6
2 horses, each		3	
3 Corporalls, each		3	
2 Trumpeters each		2	6
A Sadler		2	6
A Farrier		2	6
Souldiers Harquebusiers, each			

Dragons.

	lib.	sol.	den.
Colonell	1	10	
Serjeant Major		9	
Quartermaster		5	
Preacher		4	
Provost Marshall		5	
Chirurgeon		4	
		2	6
2 Mates, each		15	
Captain		1	
5 horses, each		4	
Lieutenant		1	
3 horses, each		3	
Cornet		1	
2 horses, each		1	6
2 Serjeants, each		1	
a horse, each		1	
3 Corporalls, each		1	
3 horses (for each, one) each		1	
2 Drums, each		1	
their horses, each		1	
A Farrier		1	
his horse		1	6
Souldiers Dragoneers, each			

Advance money to the Officers.

To the Provost Marshall for irons	7 pounds
Minister for provision and necessaries	20 pounds
Chirurgeons chest	15 pounds
Minister and Chirurgeon for their Waggon	40 pounds
To the Captain	140 pounds
Lieutenant	60 pounds
Cornet	50 pounds
Quartermaster	30 pounds
Three Corporalls, each	1 pounds
2 Trumpeters, 1 Farrier, 1 Sadler, each	8 pounds

Every Waggon at 40 pounds, or 4 shillings 8 pence per diem for every Waggon. (fix two)

The Captains of Foot have 40 pounds for a Waggon, and 10 shillings a man to raise their Companies.

Officers, Artificers, and Attendants of the Train of Artillery, consisting of 36 Pieces.

	lib.	sol.	den.
Generall of the Ordnance	4 pounds		
Lieutenant Generall	1 po. 10 shil		
Assistant		6 shill. pen.	
		2	6
2 Clerks, each		2	6
A Surveyer or Controller		10	
2 Clerks, each		2	6
Chief Engineer		10	
A Clerk		2	6
6 Engineers for ordering trenches, fortifications and approches, each		6	
6 Clerks, each		2	6
15 Guides or Conductors, each		2	
A Paymaster		5	
2 Clerks, each		2	
2 Commissaries of Ordnance, Matrosses, and Ammunition, each		5	
2 Clerks, each		2	
20 Gemtlemen of the Ordnance, each		4	
A Commissary to distribute victuall		6	
2 Clerks attending him, each		2	
A Purveyer generall for Munition and all necessaries for the Ordnance			
2 Horsemen to assist him, each		2	6
A Waggon-master for the Artillery		5	
2 Assistants, each		2	6
		2	
20 Conductors attending him, each		2	
A principall Conductor for the Artillery for draught horses and ammunition		4	
A Commissary for the train of Artillery for the draught horses		4	
Quartermaster for the train of Artillery		6	
Master of the Miners		4	
25 other Miners, each		1	
3 Captains to 600 Pioners, each		5	
3 Lieutenants, each		3	
3 Overseers of the Pioners work, each		2	
2 Petardeers or fireworkers, each		4	
to each of them 4 attendants, each		6	8
One Master Gunner		6	
3 Master Gunners mates, each		2	
20 Gunners, each		1	6
30 Gunners, each		1	
200 Labourers, each		1	
A Provostmarshall of the Artillery		3	
3 under Jaylours, each		1	5
A Battery-master		5	
A Bridge-master, with 100 Matrosses to work about rivers		6	
An Assistant to him		3	6
Every Matrosse		1	
A Chaplain		5	
An Ensigne		1	6
A Drumme		3	
A Trumpet		4	
A Chirurgeon		4	6
2 under barber Chirurgeons, each		2	
Master Carpenter		4	
2 Mates, each		2	6
24 Carpenters, each		4	
A Master Blacksmith			

	s	d		s	d
2 Mates, each	2		A Basketmaker for gabions, hurdles, baskets	2	6
6 Servants under him, each	1	6	4 Servants, each	1	6
A Master Wheelwright	3		A Collar-maker	2	6
2 Mates, each	2		4 Servants, each	1	6
8 Servants under him, each	1	6	A Ladle-maker	2	6
A Master Farrier	3		2 Servants, each	1	6
6 Servants being workmen, each	1	6	A Gunsmith	3	6
600 Pioners, each	1		2 Servants, each	2	
3 Tent-keepers, each	1	6	A Cooper	2	6
9 Servants under them, each	1		4 Servants, each	1	6
An Armourer	3		A Ropemaker	2	6
4 Servants under him, each	2		2 Servants, each	1	6

Chap. 19. *line* 34. *for* 81. *reade* 18. *Chap.* 28. *line* 30. *for* uneven, *reade* even.

Chap. 29. The horseman (having spanned his pistol) is not to return his spanner to the side of his Case (where some would have it) for there it is neither sure nor readily returned: but is to wear it in a string hanging on his left shoulder, by his right side. And for lading his Pistols (and so for the Carbine) I would (by no means) have him to use his flask, but the (farre readier) way of Cartouches, which his Holsters must always be furnished with, besides those which he is to have in store.

Chap. 32. The custome now is to make the horse but three in file for fight, so consequently divers of the motions shewed in this Chapter will be uselesse.

PART III. *Chap.* 2. Concerning Encamping, the Reader may receive more satisfaction in my book of *Castrametation*, published *Anno* 1642.

Chap. 6. and 7. And for the Watches also, in my *Order of Military Watches*, then published.

PART IIII. *Chap.* 6. and 8. The manner of fighting used by the horse (in divers Armies) now a dayes, is not by wheeling off (as formerly) but by charging through. Every man having his drawn sword in his bridle-hand, fires his Carbine or Pistol: the Carbine at 12. or 15. foot distance, and the Pistol so near as hath been shewed before in *Part* 1. *Chap.* 29. the Carbine levelled at the knees of the enemies horse, because the powder naturally, and also the least motion of the horse, use to raise the muzzle of the piece. Having fired, he presently is to betake him to his sword (unlesse the enemy by wheeling off. gives him leasure and opportunity to use his second Pistoll) and so to charge him on the flank or rear, and to fight at his best advantage. To this end, the Officers must be very carefull to exercise their Troops frequently, especially in a regimentall way (as the sole means, under God, to make them victorious) observing to keep their Troops close serried; to leave fit distances between each Troop, Regiment, and Brigade; to relieve each other orderly; to retreat(upon occasion) in due order into their appointed intervalls, and to avoid confusion.

To his much honoured Friend,
Captain *John Crufo.*

I Know the Authours works and name,
Great Mars his fcholar, is his fame:
Whofe valour, honour, induftrie
Hath taught the ufe of Cavalhy,
Accommodating thefe our times,
Surmounting th' limits of all lines,
Examples fet for imitation,
Then love to fight by Regulation:
But have not fuch been ill requited,
Whom profit never yet invited?
But blame not fuch as fteer at th' Helm
Whofe care is to preferve this Realm,
Settle Religion, Law, and Right,
Supprest by rebells force, and might.
   If ignorance or malice have
The Authours worth laid in a grave,
Wifdomes grace in men of parts
Will raife it up with tongues and hearts.
   Let none be troubled if not us'd,
When Confcience tells they ne'r abus'd;
God grant's no ufe of Marfhall men,
Till we know how to ufe; not when
Good fervice done th' age being cold
Prepar'd are new, cafheer'd are old.

Your devoted Friend,

EDMUND HARVY, Colonel

MILITARIE INSTRUCTIONS
for the
CAVALLRIE.

The firſt Part.

THE ARGUMENT.

AVALLRIE, ſo called of [a] *Cavallo*, (which in the *Italian* and *Spaniſh* ſignifieth a *horſe*) is worthily eſteemed a moſt noble and neceſſary part of the militarie profeſſion : which being the ſubject of my diſcourſe, it may be reduced to theſe foure heads.

[b] 1 The *levying* of men,
   2 Their *marching*,
   3 Their *encamping*,
   4 Their *embattelling*.

In the *levying* of men, there be two things conſiderable; 1. The *election of officers*. 2. The *election of ſouldiers*. Concerning the *officers*, they may be conſidered, 1. In *generall*, 2. In *particular*.

[a] Derived from the Latine word *Caballus*, and this from the Greek word καβάλλης.

[b] *Primùm idoneos eligamus, &c. dein & in itinere, & in cæſtris, & in præliis ipſis inſtructum exercitium habeamus;* Ælianus de inſtruendis acie bus, cap. 3.

CHAP. I.

Of officers in generall.

AS in politique government, ſo in this militarie profeſſion, every man by a naturall impreſſion is ready to conceive himſelf to be fit to command and govern others, though he never knew how to obey; whereas in every mechanicall trade or manufacture, an apprenticehood is firſt paſſed in the learning of it, before it be profeſſed and exerciſed. In this profeſſion of arms ([c] an art obtained with greateſt difficulty, and practiſed with moſt danger) men would be *Captains* before they be *ſouldiers*. And hereof the chief cauſe is ignorance, the fruitfull mother of all errours. For ſurely, if their end and aim were honour, and they knew how frail and mutable the eſtate of a ſouldier is; and that in a moment a man may loſe all the reputation obtained by many years induſtrie ; ([d] the errours in warre admitting no amendment, as in other profeſſions; but carrying their preſent puniſhment with them) and had they ſeen many ſhamefully chaſed from the army, and proclaimed infamous; and others paſſe through the hands of the hangman; they would (doubtleſſe) ſtrive with much induſtry and diligence to enable themſelves, before they came to undertake the exerciſe of ſo dangerous an employment. And they are not a little miſtaken, which think their [e] birth a ſufficient pretence to places of honour, without any qualification or merit; there being other things more reall and eſſentiall [f] required in an officer ; namely, *Knowledge, experience, valour, dexteritie*, &c.

  To be under command for a time, depreſſeth thoſe vehement paſſions which nature exciteth, eſpecially in young men, which would be very dangerous in a chief or commander. Moreover, it accuſtometh a man to danger, and [g] maketh him couragious; ſo as being ſuddainly aſſailed, he can recollect himſelf without aſtoniſhment; a moſt neceſſary thing in a commander. Adde to this, that by uſing himſelf to travell and labour, watching, hunger, thirſt, rain, and froſt; and by [h] an orderly aſcent (by degrees) from a Corporall to a Quartermaſter, from thence to a Cornet, and ſo to a Lieutenant, he prepareth himſelf for a Captains charge. He learneth the trick of entertaining his ſouldiers, and to keep them in good affection and reverence towards him. He knows their ſeverall diſpoſitions and ſufficiencies, and accordingly entruſteth them with employments. Honour muſt be his chief end ; to attain which, he muſt be very vigilant not to loſe [i] any occaſion of any brave exploit : by which means he will be alwayes obſerving his enemy, ſtudying how to prevent him or endammage him; alwayes bearing in mind this maxime , That in warre no great or remarkable matter can be effected without danger and diligence. To this end, let him be ſure to take heed that he [k] truſt not too much to his own judgement and valour, without acquainting his officers with his counſels. And let him ſo know the ſeverall inclinations and ſufficiencies of his ſouldiers, as to take particular notice of ſuch as deſerve well, and to reward them accordingly; and to rid himſelf of baſe and debauched fellows and cowards.

  He muſt alwayes aſpire (in way of [l] virtuous emulation) to higher degrees of honour. [m] Cove

[c] Le plus relevé, le plus haſardeux, & le plus difficile ſubject du monde. Le meſtier des Nobles, la pratique des courageux, & l'exercice des Princes & des Roys; Monſieur Praiſſac.

[d] In aliis rebus ſi quid erratum eſt, poteſt poſtmodum corrigi: Præliorum delictis emendationem non recipiunt, cùm pœna ſtatim ſequatur errorem; Cato apud Vegetium, lib. 1. cap. 13.

[e] Non repellitur imperator pauper ſi cum virtute ſit, quanquam claris ac illuſtribus majoribus ortus non ſit ; Leo. Tact. cap. 2. 15.

[f] In legitimo duce quinque hæc requiro ; Scientiam, virtutem, providentiam, autoritatem, fortunam; Lipſ. polit. lib. 5. cap. 15.

[g] Scientia vel bellica dimicandi nutrit audaciam; Veg. lib. 1. c. 15.

[h] Mars is therefore called Gradivus (as Feſtus hath it) quia gradatim, & per ordinem, & per or

toufnefſe he muſt hate; for nothing will better continue his ſouldiers good affections towards him then liberalitie. Gaming he muſt deteſt. [n] In ſtead of coſtly apparell, let him delight in good arms and horſes; wherein oftentimes both his life and honour conſiſteth. He muſt be continent and ſober, not given to luxurie nor [o] drunkenneſſe, but alwayes be as a good example to his ſouldiers: for otherwiſe he cannot have that requiſite libertie to chaſtiſe them for thoſe vices which his own conſcience will accuſe himſelf to be guiltie of.

Above all, let him ſet before his eyes (as the originall and foundation of all perfection) the fear of God; carrying himſelf (ſo farre as may be) internally and externally inculpable. For the horrour of a guiltie conſcience, and the imminent danger and apprehenſion of death meeting together, take away all courage and valour. And thus having reformed himſelf, he ſhall the more eaſily reform his ſouldiers, and make them fit for every honourable enterpriſe.

n The States edict of Marſhall law provideth, that ſuch as in their drunkenneſſe ſhall commit any offence, ſhall not therefore be any way excuſed, but the more ſeverely puniſhed; Art. 69.

n Philopæmenes pubent ad ſe armandum impulit, deinde delicias & luxum eorum optimè moeritis. Omnes inflammavit, ut quotidianis repreſſis in corpos ſumptibus, geſtiens in militari & bellico ornatu oſtentareſe ſplendidos. Profuſio impenſa in hujuſmodi rei, robora animum, extolliſque; Plutarch, in Philop.

CHAP. II.

Of Officers in particular.

Of the Generall of horſe.

TOuching the particular officers, the [p] Generall of the horſe, as being one of the principall Chiefs of an army, muſt be a ſouldier of extraordinary experience and valour; having in charge the nerve of the principall forces, and on whom the good ſucceſſe of many deſignes and actions dependeth, as being moſt uſually executed by the Cavallrie, eſpecially in battels: where the charging of the enemie in good order uſually giveth victorie; and contrarywiſe, the [q] diſorders of the Cavallrie often diſturb and disband the whole armie. The Generall of the horſe was wont to ſupplie the place of Lieutenant Generall of the army, and in the Lord Generalls abſence to command the whole armie. True it is, that the Lord Marſhall, foraſmuch as he giveth the orders, uſed to have ſome ſuperioritie of command, according to the opinions of ſome; whence it cometh that the Lord Generall, abſenting himſelf from the armie, uſed to take along with him either the Generall of horſe, or the Lord Marſhall, to avoid the occaſions of competition. It is his office to take particular notice not onely of the Captains and officers, but alſo of thoſe private ſouldiers which are carefull and punctuall in their ſervice, [r] rewarding and honouring them in publick when they perform ſome ſignall act, and advancing them to offices without partialitie. On the other ſide, [s] he muſt chaſtiſe delinquents, and ſuch as are wanting in their endeavours: by which means he ſhall be reverenced and loved of good men, and feared of ſuch as are bad. It belongeth to his care, that the Cavallrie be in good equipage, and fitted with all neceſſaries requiſite: And that the companies (being to march) be provided of nags; without which the ſouldiers can hardly preſerve their horſe of ſervice, by reaſon that with them they muſt go to forrage (for want of bidets or nags) after their march, and preſently enter into guard in the armie or quarter, without any reſt to refreſh their horſes. He is not to ſuffer the Captains either to make officers, or to abſent themſelves from their companies, without his leave and approbation. He hath his officers apart, and in that which concerneth the Cavallrie, neither the Lord Marſhall, nor Lord Generall himſelf uſeth to diſpoſe of any thing without his advice. If he paſſe among the quarters of Cavallrie, or Infanterie, his trumpets are to ſound; but not where the Lord Generall lodgeth, or where he is in perſon. When he commandeth in the armie (in abſence of the Lord Generall) upon occaſion of fight, his place is in the battel, that he may be able to give order to all. He hath uſually a companie (heretofore of lances) to lodge with him, and to ſerve him as his guard; having uſually ſix ſouldiers or more of his companie attending on him. [u] He ſhould not reſolve upon any enterpriſe, unleſſe he firſt conſider ſeriouſly of all that might happen; that ſo, propounding to himſelf greater difficulties in the action, then in effect they be, he may prepare remedies ſurpaſſing all the ſaid difficulties: it being a benefit not to be expreſſed, to be able to [x] foreſee (with good judgement) thoſe things which might ſucceed in the uncertain and variable accidents of warre. Eſpecially he muſt be [y] ready in execution: for ſuppoſe a determination never ſo well grounded, yet it may prove vain and hurtfull, if it be not executed with requiſite promptitude.

p Iphicrates, reſembled an army to a mans body; calling the heavy armed the body, the light armed the hands, the horſe the feet; and the Generall the head; Plutarch.
q Witneſſe the battel of Gemblours, deſcribed by Meteren. lib. 8. where the Infanterie is overthrown by their own horſe. So did the Burgundians; Les hommes d'armes Bourguignons rompirent leurs propres Archers; Phil. de Comines. lib. 1. cap. 3.
r Perſcutaborh qui ſe in bello ſtrenuè geſſerint, illiſq; ignavos anium qui par eſt ſupplicia conſtringes; Leo. Tact. cap. 16.
ſ Monſieur de la Nolle reporteth that (in his time) in the regiment of Colonel Pedro de Pas (conſiſting of 23 companies of Spaniards) there was more then 3200 crowns a moneth given for extraordinary ſervices and ſignall acts.

Whence he draweth this obſervation, Qui eſt un bon teſmoignage quil eſtoit rempli d'hommes valeureux, Diſcourſe Polit. & Milit. t Omnes culpæ legibus vindicet, nulli erranium credatur ignoſcens; Veg. lib. 3. cap. 10. u Of Ceſar it is ſaid, Dubium cautior an audentior. Suet. A good Commander ſhould rather look behind him then before him, ſaid Sertorius. Plutarch, in Serter. x Tonuritas, praeterquam quòd ſtulta eſt, etiam infelix; Livius 22. y Intentus ſis, ut neque tua occaſioni deſit, neque ſuam hoſti des. Ibid.

CHAP. III.

Of the Lieutenant Generall of horſe.

THe charge of the Lieutenant Generall of the horſe hath ever been held of very great importance; and therefore muſt be ſupplied by a perſon of great experience and valour; one that muſt be very carefull and diligent, becauſe he uſually marcheth and lodgeth with the Cavallrie. For which cauſe he ought to be well verſed in the opportunitie of the wayes, upon occaſion of meeting the enemie in marching.   He

He must alwayes have his thoughts busied about the motions of the enemie, discoursing with himself from what part they might shew themselves, with what number of men, whether with Infanterie or not, in how many houres they might come upon him from their armie or garrison, and whether they might present themselves in a place of advantage; that so it might be prevented, as need should require.

He must also advisedly choose commodious places for the quarters or lodgings, providing good guards, causing the highwayes to be scoured or discovered, placing men on those passages where the enemie might make head, not neglecting to send out rounders, and omitting no diligence to secure the quarter in which the Cavallrie findeth it self exposed to greater dangers then can befall it any other way, especially being lodged without Infanterie.

He must also procure to have spies, not onely in the enemies armie, but also upon their frontiers, to penetrate their designes and intentions, omitting no inventions which may stand him in stead to avoid inconveniences; knowing that diligence is the mother of good fortune. His particular care is to see that the Captains wrong not their souldiers, that they keep their companies in good state and well armed, and that themselves and their officers do their endeavours, and observe good order and discipline.

Towards the souldiers he must be no lesse affable, and ready to heare them willingly in their just complaints, and to help them in their necessities, then rigorous in punishing.

He should also (himself being free from covetousnesse) give order to others to use no extortion, whereby the countrey is ruined, and the souldier made odious, to the prejudice of the Prince his service; it being evident that too great a liberty of the souldiers produceth nothing but very bad effects.

Upon divers occasions of sending a good part of the Cavallrie to divers places, the charge is given to the Lieutenant Generall; not onely of the horse, but also of the foot which accompanie them, according to the occurrences: for which cause he must also know how to command the Infanterie.

In absence of the Generall the whole weight resteth upon him; and to him are the orders sent from the Lord Generall or Lord Marshall, and to him (as Chief) reports are made of all the occurrences of the Cavallrie.

He may sequester a Captain from his companie, upon just cause and demerit; but cannot restore him without order from the Generall, who first gives notice thereof to the Lord Generall.

He was wont to have a companie of lances, which usually were lodged near his person; whereof foure souldiers always attend him. When he passeth by the quarters of Cavallrie the trumpets sound, but not in the Generalls quarter, or where he is. When the Generall of horse commandeth the whole armie, and therefore takes his place (in fight) in the battel, the Lieutenant Generall placeth himself in the vanguard of the Cavallry, where otherwise the Generall useth to be.

CHAP. IIII.

Of the Commissarie Generall.

THe Commissarie Generall commandeth in the absence of the Lieutenant Generall, and therefore must be a man of great experience. This charge was first instituted by *Don Ferrand de Gonzagua*, afterward continued by the Duke of *Alva*, and confirmed by the Duke of *Parma*, and so remained. He must be vigilant, and carefull to appease dissentions which grow among the souldiers, as he which dealeth most with them. He is to send and distribute the orders, and keep record of the lists of the guards, convoyes, and other services. He is to go every evening to receive the orders and the word; and having given it to the Generall and Lieutenant Generall, he is to give it to the Quartermaster Generall, that he may distribute it. Sometime he hath a companie of harquebusiers given him, in acknowledgement of his merit, not as annexed to his place. In all actions he is of singular use, entrusted especially with the execution of the orders. In appointing the lodgings, or places in severall exploits, he must be free from partialitie; and such as at this time have cause of discontent, he must make amends the next; that so they may see it was of necessitie, not of partialitie. His place is of very great use and importance, as will appear throughout this discourse.

CHAP. V.

Of the Quartermaster Generall.

THe Quartermaster Generall must be a man of great dexteritie and diligence, and well experienced in Cavallrie. It is his office to appoint the lodgings or quarterings; wherefore he must well know the countrey, the villages and places, where to place the corps-du-gards, and sentinells, and what wayes must be scoured. He is to keep a list of the guards, convoyes, cavalcadoes (or exploits by horse) &c. He must visit the guards and sentinells by day and night, and must

positio, valli & fossa destinatio pertinebat. Tabernacula vel casa militum, cum impedimentis omnibus manu ipsius curabantur; Veget. lib. 2. cap. 11.

B 2 shew

Marginal notes:

a *Erat Philopœmen præcipua in ducendo agmine locisque capiendis solertia atque usus. Nec bellorum temporibus, sed etiam in pace ad id maximè animum exercebat. Ubi iter quopiam faceret, & ad difficilem transitu saltum venisset, contemplabatur ab omni parte loci naturam, cum solus iret, secum ipse agitabat animo; cum comites habebat, ab iis quærebat, si hostis eo loco apparuisset, quid si à fronte, quid si à latere hoc aut illo, quid si à tergo adoriretur, capiendum consilii foret: T. Livius dec. 4. lib. 5.*

b *Cui enim cura præcipua insignis tribuimur, cujus fidei integ. virtutis possessionum fortuna, tutela vitam, salus militum, reipublica creditur, loricatus non tantum pro universo exercitu, sed etiam pro singulis contubernalibus debet esse solicitus. Veg. l. 3. cap. 10.*

c Extortions (of divers kinds) are punishable with death, by the edict of Marshall law, published by the States of the united provinces; Anne 4.

a The Romanes were very exact in keeping records and lists of their forces, watches, duties, payes, &c. *Quotidianas (tam in pace) vigilias; item excubitum sive agmina de omnibus centuriis & contubernalis, qua vicissim milites faciunt; ut ne qua contra justitiam prægravetur, aut alieni præstetur immunitas: nomina eorum qui vices suas fecerunt, brevibus inseruntur. Veg. lib. 2 cap. 19.*

a This officer among the Romanes was called Præfectus castrorum. *Ad quem castrorum lib. 2. cap. 11.*

shew the allarm-place to the particular Quartermasters, when they go to him in the evening to receive the word. He must (by ᵇ maps or otherwise) be well informed of the countrey , knowing the qualitie and bignesse of every village, and their distance one from another, obtaining from the Marshall of the field some one of the countrey to inform him. He must be true in his reports, and if any order (for haste) be given him by word of mouth, himself must go and deliver it, and not trust it to others. On the Spanish side, in the Low-countrey warres: the Quartermaster Generall hath two assistants allowed him, to help to discharge the travells of his office; but on the States side that service is performed by the particular Quartermasters.

CHAP. VI.
Of the Captain.

Since that the ᵃ Captains places have been disposed of by the Prince (as the Captains in Flanders are appointed at the Court of Spain) there are grown these two inconveniences upon it. First, young and unexperienced gentlemen are made Captains. Secondly, many good souldiers are lost, which seeing their hopes of advancement by degrees and merit cut off, abandon the service. Whereas the charge of a Captain of horse is of so great importance and qualitie in the army, as it should not be given to any, but to men of singular valour and experience; for often it falleth out, that of themselves, without orders or counsel of any other (as occasion requireth) they must execute services of great weight and consequence. ᵇ He must be vigilant, sober, continent, modest in his apparell, curious to have good horses and arms, thereby to give example to his souldiers, and to see them punctuall in their service, and exactly observant of discipline; for their excursions and extortions cannot be remedied, unlesse the Captain keep them in order: wherein if he be negligent, he looseth his reputation with his superiours. If he be covetous or given to gaming, he is ready to be drawn to lay hands (oftentimes)on the pay due to the souldiers; whereby he also overthroweth his reputation and credit. A covetous desire of riches should not enter into a generous heart. He must diligently and punctually observe the orders which shall be given or sent him from his superiours, and be in the place at the appointed houre with his companie, and others under his charge. On all occasions he must be first on horseback, and keep his company full and compleat. He must alwayes strive by desert to advance himself to higher places, always studying how to endammage his enemy; to this end he ought often to ᶜ consult with his best experienced souldiers. He must endeavour to know every one of his souldiers by their ᵈ names, that so he may distinctly name them upon occasion of employment; it being an encouragement to them to be known by name of their Captain. Whatsoever should befall, he must ᵉ take heed of discovering any fear, on whose courage and countenance the souldiers depend, and must alwayes shew a good resolution in the orders which he shall give, without confounding himself; knowing that there is no place for counsel in him, who hath his discourse of reason seazed by fear. He must ᶠ cherish his well deserving souldiers, and cashiere the contrary; and it must be his care to have one or more of his souldiers well ᵍ skilled in the wayes of the country, to serve him as guides : (because the boors are neither alwayes at hand, nor alwayes to be trusted) and to such he is to give some allowance extraordinary. Out of his company he is to choose his Lieutenants, Cornets, &c. weighing onely every ones merit, without any passion; whereby he shall give content and encouragement to his souldiers, and shall be sure not to be crossed by the Generall in the confirmation of the said officers.

The charge of the troops used to be given to the Captains of lances, as having a prerogative above other Captains of horse, or to the eldest Captain : yet the Chief ought to have regard to their sufficiency for command, and to give the charge to them that are ablest to perform it.

In absence of the Captains of lances (when they were in use)the Captains of cuirassiers commanded; and in their absence, the Captains of harquebusiers. The Lieutenants observed the same rules.

CHAP. VII.
Of the Lieutenant.

IT is necessary, that the Lieutenant of a troop of horse be a man of abilitie and experience, nourished and educated in Cavallrie. To this office such were usually raised, which (for their deserts) had been Corporalls and Cornets.

ᵃ In the Captains absence he commandeth the company, upon whom usually all difficulties do rest ; because (oft times) the companies are given to young gentlemen which want experience. He must be strict in seeing the souldiers do their service with all fitting punctualitie, and to have a care of their horses and arms. ᵇ He alwayes marcheth in the rear of the companie, causing the souldiers to follow the Captain and Standard (or Cornet) in good order, well closed together, and to suffer none to depart from the troop. Upon occasion of fight he is still to be on the rear with his sword drawn, encouraging the souldiers, and killing any that shall offer to flie or disband: but in case of the Captains absence, he shall take the Captains place, appointing an officer to be in the rear. In the ordinary marching of the company, or passing by some place, or going to the

allarm

allarm-place, or to the parado, the Lieutenant must not take the Captains place, but march in the rear, because the lances and cuirassiers have their Cornets to lead them at the head of the company. Among the harquebusiers the Lieutenant was wont to take the Captains place, (according to *Melzo* and *Basta*) because then they had no [c] Cornets; but these last warres having given them Cornets, the rule holdeth for them as for the lances and cuirassiers.

[d] He must of necessitie be able to write and reade, because he keepeth the list of the names and sirnames of the souldiers of the companie; and by reason of orders or letters sent to him from his superiours, which he must not shew to others. He must know the sufficiencie of every souldier, and upon occasion make use of them accordingly.

The company going to the guard in any place, and approching near it, the Lieutenant goeth before to take notice of the Corps-du-guard, and speaking with the Lieutenant of the company which is to change, informeth himself by him of the place, of the sentinells for day and night, what wayes he must scoure, and of all other things requisite. He must himself go and place the sentinells, visiting them often, and using all diligence, keeping himself alwayes armed, (at least with the breast and cask) and his horse bridled, when he hath the guard.

The company being lodged in some village, he must cause the billets to be signed by the Quartermaster of his company, to be distributed to the souldiers before the Cornets lodging, where the Alto is made to attend the said billets; that so (in case of an allarm) the souldiers may know where to assemble together at their Cornet.

If they stay longer then a day in one place, the Lieutenant is to visit the houses, to see good rule kept by the souldiers; and being to march away, to command them carefully to put out their fires. Going to be lodged in a town or fort, there to keep their garrison, the Lieutenant must accommodate their lodgings according to their degrees and deserts. And wheresoever they lodge longer then a day, he must write the names of the souldiers on the said billets, and keep a register of them; that so upon any complaint of their hostes, it may be easily remedied , by the ready finding and punishing of the delinquents.

When the company is to march, and the trumpets sound to horse, he [e] must be first ready and mounted, having care that all the souldiers immediately do the same. And if he find any lingering, either of lazinesse, or with a purpose to stay behind to pillage the houses, he must chastise them with all severity, for example to others. He must have knowledge of the countrey and wayes, being often sent upon exploits where the guides are not alwayes ready. If the company be charged by the enemy, the Lieutenant, with some of the best mounted souldiers, is to remain behind.

emptiom, &c. *Ipse manu sua pila gerens, præcedit anheli Militis ora pedes: monstrat tolerare labores, Non jubet; —— Lucan. 9. de Catone.*

CHAP. VIII.
Of the Cornet.

THe Cornet of horse must be couragious. In absence of the Captain and Lieutenant he commandeth the company. His place of march is in the front, before the first rank, yet behinde the Captain. In fight, the Cornet of lances used to march even with the Captain, upon his left hand; and charging with him, strove to break the standard upon his enemy; which being so broken and falling to the ground, [a] he was not to regard to get it up again (especially not to alight for it.) If he were to charge a flying enemy (whether horse or foot) he was also to assay to break his standard.

The Cornet of cuirassiers in march hath his place at the head of the company, and also presenteth himself in the allarm-place; but in fight he is to be in the middle of the troop, leaving ¾ parts of the souldiers behind him: [b] those before him must be of the best armed, and most couragious. He must also keep a list of the company, to send so many to the guard as the Captain or Lieutenant shall appoint. Once a day, at the Lord Generalls first passing by the troop, he is to do obeysance, by inclining the cornet towards the ground.

so long as he could, then wound himself in his colours and died; *Mendoza. lib.4.*   But if the enemy should get the cornet unbroken, then it were a great disgrace; *Basta lib.4.*   [b] *Optimus cuiusque decus in præpone, & duetor cæterorum omnium esse debet;* Ælian. cap. 5.   *Cavendum, ut etiam æquum servendum multo comitu idoneos;* Ibid. cap. 13.   The reason is, because the first rank being the edge, it must be made good by the second and the rest, if occasion be.

CHAP. IX.
Of the particular Quartermasters.

THe [a] particular Quartermasters should be men so qualified, as reasonably they might pretend the Cornet, and (in absence of the Cornet) might command the company. When all the companies are lodged together, they accompany the Quartermaster Generall in making the quarters: but being to be lodged in severall places (as often it happeneth) some accompany the Lieutenant Generall, others the Commissary Generall. Where a Captain commandeth the quarter, the particular Quartermaster of that respective company maketh the quarter. There is much fidelity required in them, in consideration of distributing the word, and the billets. They use also to distribute the souldiers pay, in the King of Spains warres; but on the States side the clerks of the

Mensores sive mensuratores præmittes, qui castrorum ambitum, in quo castra ponentur, dimetiuntur; & certam quandam mensuram cum proportione justa unicuiq; turma tribuant; Leo Tact. cap. 9. 7.

Marginal notes:

c As the *Velites* among the Romanes, *qui nec signa propria habuere, nec duces*; Lips. ad Polyb. lib. 2.

d The Romanes required it in their private souldiers, and to cast account also. *In quibusdam nostrum peritis, calculandi computandique usu exiguus* Veg. lib. 2. cap. 19.

e The good example of a Leader hath ever been observed to be of marvellous efficacy, according to that of the Poet, —— *Componitur orbis Regis ad ex-*

a This is contrary to the use of Infantery, among which the preserving of the colours hath ever been prized above lifes as appeared (among others) by one *Jaques Marieu* who finding himself forsaken by most of the souldiers, fought

a The particular Quartermasters, the Romanes called *Metatores,* Veg. lib. 2. cap. 7. Also *Mensores, qui in castris ad podismum dimetiuntur loca, in quibus milites tentoria figant, vel hospitia in civitatibus præstiant;* Ibid.

company onely meddle with the souldiers pay, and account to their Captain; having a cuirassiers pay, and being exempted from bearing arms, or doing the duties of a souldier.

In going with the Quartermaster Generall to make the lodgings, the Quartermaster must be very diligent, taking with him one or two souldiers (such as the Lieutenant shall appoint him) which shall return to their company, and conduct them to their quarter.

CHAP. X.
Of the Corporalls.

COrporalls are very usefull in a troop of horse. They must assist the Lieutenant in placing the sentinells, when the souldiers of their particular squadron are to perform that service.

The harquebusiers are usually sent to discover or scoure the high-wayes, and to be forerunners or scouts, under the charge of one of their Corporalls; [a] for which respects he must be a man of experience. Some passage or place of importance being to be guarded, a Corporall is sent thither with his squadron. He must be able to write and reade, keeping a list of his squadron. The Captain alloweth him half a place of fortage, and a share of 10. *per cent.*

a Mistakes in such as are sent ont to discover, do often bring much trouble upon the army, and shame upon themselves. A memorable example hereof is recorded by *Phil. de Comines*, of the *Burgundians*, who taking a field of great thistles to be a grosse of their enemies lanciers, reported it so to their Chiefs, and caused a great hurly-burly in the whole army; *Lib.*1.*cap.*11.

CHAP. XI.
Of the Trumpeters.

IT is not enough that a Trumpeter know how (exactly) to sound all the severall sounds of the trumpet, but he must also be discreet and judicious; not onely to be fit to deliver embassies and messages as they ought, but (at his return) to [a] report what he hath observed concerning the enemies works and guards, and what he hath further gathered and spied. To do this, he must be wittie and subtile, knowing how to invent and affirm things which are not, artificially concealing whatsoever passeth among those of his own side. He must sound the [b] *boutezselle* precisely at the houre appointed him; and when the Cornet giveth him the list of the guards, he must signifie it unto them. One Trumpeter must alwayes lodge with the Cornet, to whom the Captain is to give means for his entertainment. He must alwayes have his trumpet about him, to have it ready at a sudden allarm.

a *Ne mi nco si lasci troppo usare la frequentia di venire trombetti & tamburri: perche in quel' essercito tall' hora son huomini molto astuti & pratichi; da potervi nocere assai;* G. Catanen. di fortif. &' cap. 4.   b That is, *set on the saddle*; being the first sound when the horse are to march; the next is *a chevall*, that is, *mount on horseback*; the third and last is a *standart*, that is, *repair to your Cornet.* See chap. 32.

CHAP. XII.
Of the Auditor.

ON the Spanish side in the Low-countreys, the Cavallrie have an Auditor by themselves; who must be a man of great integritie, well seen in the laws, and of great practice. In the absence of the Auditor Generall, he supplieth his place. He heareth and judgeth the causes of the Cavallrie, and maketh report of all that passeth to the Generall, or the Lieutenant Generall in his absence; without whose order he cannot execute any of his sentences. The Cavallrie lying in garrison, he condemneth not to death, without reporting first to the Lord Generall and Auditor Generall. He is to keep near the person of the Generall or Lieutenant Generall, who are to see him duely respected. He is to take notice of the prices of victuall which are brought to the quarter of horse, that they be sold at a reasonable rate; and to see that the victuallers suffer no extortion by the Provost Marshall or his officers.

But in the States army, the horse and foot have but one Auditor or Fiscall Generall; who passeth no sentence himself, but that is done by the [a] Councel of Warre, wherein every Captain hath a voice.

a The Councel of Warre among the Romanes, consisted of their Legates, Questors, Tribanes, and the Centurions: *Convocato concilio, &c. omninumque ordinum adhibitis centurionibus;* Caesar Com. lib.1. cap.16.

CHAP. XIII.
Of the Provost Marshall.

OF all things in the charge of the Provost Marshall, his principall care must be about the victualls. He must be an honest man, and content with his fees. He is to look to the weights and measures and to guard the victuallers (or sutlers) from insolencies. Himself or some of his men must alwayes be in the market-place, or where the victualls are sold; and he is to inform himself where and at what price the sutlers buy their victuall, that the Commissarie and Auditor may tax them accordingly. He must cause the orders to be strictly observed which shall be published in the horse-quarters: and those quarters must he purge of rogues and thieves. He must alwayes carry his staffe or truncheon in his hand, (the badge of his office) and having the same, [a] it is death

a See the States edi:9, Art. 78.

for

for any souldier any way to lay hands on him. If he be to take a prisoner, he must not enter the quarter without leave of the Chief, but the Chief is to cause the delinquent to be delivered to him. But if the offence be hainous, so as the delinquent is like to run away for it, he may (of his own authority) enter any quarter; but not carry the prisoner away without license of the Chief of that quarter. In marching, he is to clear the by-wayes of straggling souldiers, to prevent them of pillaging.

Some make it part of his charge to provide guides, and to have regard to the baggage, both for the placing of it in the quarter, as also for the safetie of it; to that end sending one of his men before, with the Quartermaster Generall, by whom the baggage may be conducted to the place assigned. But this more properly belongeth to the office and charge of the Waggon-master.

CHAP. XIIII.
Of Souldiers in generall.
Of the corruption of the Cavallrie.

SOuldiers take their name from the Dutch word **Soldye**, which signifieth *pay* or *stipend*; profit being one of the ends why men undertake the military profession, and honour not the onely (though the chiefest) of their aims. And therefore they which were of opinion, that the way to reform the Militia of Flanders, was to redouble the labours of the souldiers and shorten their pay, were much mistaken. And it will rather be found, that the scanting of the souldiers profits, and increasing their toil, procured the corruption of their Cavallrie. The honest profit of a souldier may be twofold. 1. Ordinary, which is set pay. 2. Extraordinary, which are rewards for speciall meriting services; and these are joyned with honour.

Among the Romanes, [b] the Legionary souldiers had allowance of pay, corn, and apparrell, by a decree of the Senate 349. yeares after the building of the city; having till that time served without pay, but not without many profits, and having all necessaries provided them of the publick. A horse-mans pay was then a *drachma* or *denarius* a day (of our money about 7. pence halfpeny.) In *Cesars* time it was doubled, (as [c] *Suetonius* testifieth) and *Augustus* augmented it to three *denarii* a day. They had their [d] apparell allowed them of the publick, and corn ; namely, wheat for themselves and attendants, and barley and oats for their horses, [e] being two *medimni* of wheat, and seven of barley and oats a moneth (the *medimnus* being about a bushel and an half of our measure.) They had also their shares of booties, which were very large and ample. Besides, for extraordinary rewards, they had oftentimes [f] assignments of land, of inheritance,& houses also; sufficient to maintain them without using any trades. Moreover they had rewards in money. At the triumph of [g] *Pompey* out of *Asia*, every private souldier had 1500. *drachmas*, (of our money 46. pounds 3. shillings 9. pence) and the officers in proportion. And shortly after, at the triumph of [h] *Cesar*, every souldier had 5000. *drachmas*, (which is 156. pounds 5. shillings) &c. Furthermore, [i] they had many kinds of honourable rewards for signall acts, and those bestowed in great pomp at publick assemblies of all the Commanders, by the Imperatour (or Generall) himself, and a record kept of those services. These rewards were of many kinds; as severall sorts of arms, horses, rich trappings, jewels, golden bracelets, &c. Besides, their severall sorts of crowns, as their [k] *Corona civica, obsidionalis, muralis, castrensis, vallaris, navalis, &c.* which crowns were put upon their heads in great state and solemnitie by the Generall. These they wore upon all publick occasions; as at playes, in triumphs, in judgement, &c. [l] for their military profession made them the more capable (afterwards) of offices in the administration of the Common-wealth.

If but such profits and encouragements were given to souldiers in these dayes , it were easie to keep them in good order and discipline. But what is [m] seven *Phillips dallers* (35. shillings English) a moneth for a horse-man, to maintain himself , his boy, and two horses , and that but ill paid ? whence shall he have means to provide himself apparell ? and if his horse fail, how shall he be able to buy another? And whereas a horse-man at the time when this pay was first ordered, could put himself in [n] sufficient equipage for 20. or 25. *Phillips dallers* (which is five pounds, or six pounds five shillings) now the price of all things is so raised, as he shall hardly accomplish it with 60, which is 15 pounds starling. As for extraordinary rewards they are very rare, offices usually being bestowed for favour, if not for money. So that good spirits and honest men (seeing their way of [o] advancement cut off, and considering that without pillaging and robbing they cannot live) give over the service. They which remain, infringing all discipline (many of them) [p] fall to extortion and stealing: and if an officer shall punish them for it, he giveth occasion of mutinies.

[a] *Monsieur de la Noüe* his souldiers, in service of the States, so regarded their reputation, as (after some want of pay) news being brought that it was come, and they being to receive it, they made answer. It was not then a time to take money, but to attend the exploits which they had in hand *Meter. lib.9.* [b] *Anno urbis condita 349. decreto Senatus ut stipendium milles de publico acciperet, cum ante id tempus de suo quisque functus eo munere esset.* Liv.lib.4. [c] Jul.o, cap.26. [d] *Imperatoriis milles, qui vestie & annonâ publicâ pascitur.* Veget. lib.2. cap.19. [e] Polyb. lib 6 [f] Liv.lib.3 1. [g] *Appianus* Mithrid. [h] Ibid. de bello civ. lib.2. [i] Lipsius de Milit. Rom, lib.5. ex Polyb. [k] For the severall kinds of these Crowns (both for matter and form) see figure sented in figure by *Siemechius* upon *Vegetius.* For what merits they were bestowed *Lipsius* setteth down, lib 5.de milit. Rom. [l] *Urbanum vero magistratum non ante capere calicet*

quam sat, quàm decem stipendia militia adimplerit; Polyb.   [m] A horsemans pay in the king of Spains army.   [n] The Romanes (out of the publick treasury) allowed to every horseman *dos i millis aris* (about 25 pounds sterling) to buy his horse: and *bina millia* (five pounds) to keep him, *Livius lib.1.*   [o] Thus *Meñzo* and *Basta* complained, being both Lieutenant Generalls in the king of Spains warres, in the Low countreys.   [p] *Quibus ob equitatum & flagitis, maxima peccandi necessitudo est,* Tacit. 3. Annal.

CHAP. XV.

How to reform the Cavallrie.

AS every Common-wealth is supported by reward and punishment, so to reform the Cavallrie [a](where there is need of reformation) there must be good laws, and good pay: for, to suffer a souldier to fall into want by not giving him competent maintenance, maketh him forget obedience and discipline. It were therefore better to diminish their [b] number then their profits : That done, they may easily be brought to a strict observation of discipline and obedience. The laws and articles which ought to be propounded unto them, should comprise all that is to be observed in military discipline: for brevitie sake (presupposing all good orders about the service of God, the severe chastising of blasphemers, the strict forbidding of gaming (as the occasion of waste of money, and begetting quarrels) and such like morall institutions) it shall here suffice to touch upon some few of the most necessary for the Cavallrie.

1 [c] That no Captain receive any souldiers of another company, or make any officers , without approbation of the Generall; to the end he may take notice of the quality of the person. And that such souldiers as are disabled to undergo the labour of the warre, through age, be removed to some castle, &c. and be provided of some competencie, out of dead payes, or otherwise.

2 That, to avoid the [d] trouble of much baggage, which much slackeneth the motion of the Cavallrie, no man carrie a [e] woman into the field. That no souldier have above one horse of service for his baggage, unlesse some person of qualitie , with whom the Commissarie Generall may dispense. And that no officer of a companie have a waggon, but onely the Captain, and he to have onely one.

3 That rewards and honourable recompenses be established for souldiers of speciall desert, and punishments for sluggards: in particular, about attending the Cornet and obedience to the sound of the trumpet. And that such as forsake the standard (or cornet) whilest it is advanced, be punished with death. That in fight, when the trumpet soundeth a retreat, [g] whosoever presently retireth not , be punished with severitie. And that the Captain (as oft as the Cornet entereth the Corps-du-guard) himself enter with it, all excuses set aside.

4 [h] That the souldiers be kept from straggling here and there, and have the companies ready upon all occasions : the officers are bound not to absent themselves from their companies without leave of their superiours. [i] And if any souldier depart without licence , he is to be punished with death.

5 That good order be observed about distribution of bootie ; whereof shall be treated in the chapter following.

6 [k] That mutinies be prevented : and whosoever is found to have a hand in any, is to be proclaimed infamous, and perpetually banished.

7 To the end that these (and what other orders may be thought fitting) be duly observed, the authoritie of the Captain and other officers must be established and confirmed, as also that of the Provost Marshall, according to those rules before-mentioned in the office of the Provost Marshall.

CHAP. XVI.

Of distributing bootie.

ALl [a] bootie (whether it be given by occasion of defeating the enemie, or going out upon parties, &c.) is free to them that take it, whether they be prisoners , or any thing else, the Lord Generall being in the field. But otherwise , it is to be shared among them that were employed in the action.

One part is for the Infanterie, and two for the Cavallrie : and it is death to him that shall let go any prisoner, or horse, or other bootie, or shall use any fraud whatsoever : and they that shall not discover it (knowing of any such deceit) shall loose their shares. The Captains, being present at the taking of bootie, use to have five shares, and two for two pages. The Lieutenants three, and the Cornets two, and either of them one for a page. But of later times the Captains take ten parts, the Lieutenants six, the Cornets foure , according to the places which they have in forage.

The bootie being reparted , every companie giveth 10. *per centum* to their Captain of what is gotten, though he were not present : to the chief of the troop (though but a private souldier) two parts, and so to the guides.

All the bootie being brought together, they choose two of the discreetest souldiers to cause the bootie to be sold : these keep account of the money taken for it, certifying the Chief thereof, who ordereth to every man his due proportion. The Trumpets must have leave of the chief Commander of the place to sell the said bootie, and the buyer is to give one of every twentie to the trumpeter, for his pains in the sale: which money is to be divided among the trumpeters which were employed in the taking of that bootie; they having no other share.

If one or more horses were hurt or killed in the combat; or any souldiers chanced to be hurt in the said action, those horses must be made good, and the souldiers are to be recompensed, before the bootie be divided, at the discretion of the Chief.

If any souldiers horse fall lame, after the troop be marched a good distance from the quarter, so as he be forced to return back, yet shall that souldier have his share of the bootie, as if he had been present at the taking thereof.

Moreover, concerning the taking of prisoners, because other authours are scant in this particular, it will not be amisse (for the better satisfaction of such as are not acquainted with that language) to adde something out of the States edict, as followeth.

Every souldier (of what condition soever he be) shall forthwith, and before evening, bring all such of the enemie as are taken prisoners before him, which commandeth in the quarter; upon pain of loosing his prisoner, and being punished with death.

And if any should take some eminent officer, or commander of the enemie prisoner, or other person of qualitie; they shall be bound to present the same (or cause him to be presented and delivered) immediately to the Lords the States Generall, or the Councel of State, receiving for them (as also for other prisoners which the said States shall take to themselves) some reasonable recompence, according to the qualitie or abilitie of the said prisoners; yet not exceeding the summe of 500. pounds, whereby the said prisoner shall remain at the disposing of the said States: and they which took him, ought to have no further pretence to him.

It shall not be lawfull for any man to cause a prisoner to be killed, or set at ransom: nor (after ransom be paid) to suffer him to depart, without leave of the Generall, or of him that commandeth in the quarter, on pain of being disarmed, and banished out of the provinces.

And if any prisoner be found to walk about the leaguer or place of garrison, without leave of the Generall or Commander in that quarter or garrison; the partie which had taken him shall forfeit his said prisoner, to the profit of him who first shall apprehend the said prisoner.

All lawfull booties are to be certified by the takers thereof, to the Commander of the quarter within three houres after their arrivall; and are to be registred, and sold in the open market, &c. upon pains of forfeiture, and of corporall punishment, &c.

Artic. 59.

60.

61.

62.

CHAP. XVII.

Of the Souldiers pay.

THe means to have these and other good orders duly observed, is, (as is abovesaid) by giving to the souldiers their pay in competent measure and due time. The proportion which was observed on the King of Spains side, since the end of the late truce with the States of the united Provinces, is as followeth.

The Generall of horse his pay or entertainment, is 500. crowns a moneth, besides 86½ for his companie.

The Leutenant Generall 200. and 86½ for his companie.

The Commissarie Generall 80. and the pay of a Captain of Harquebusiers, when he hath a companie.

The Captains of lances and Cuirassiers 80. and 6½ for their page.

The Lieutenant of lances and Cuirassiers 25. and 6½ for a page.

The Cornets 15. and 6½ for a page.

The souldiers of lances and Cuirassiers have 6½ crowns a moneth.

The Captains of Harquebusiers have 70. crowns a moneth, and 6. for a page.

The Lieutenant 25. and 6. for a page.

The souldiers have six crowns a moneth.

On the Spanish side they were wont to allow no Cornet to the Harquebusiers (as is elsewhere shewed) and therefore no pay is here set down for him; but that course is since altered, and his pay is onely one twelfth part inferiour to the pay of a Cornet of Cuirassiers.

Besides these stipends, there is given to every companie 10. *per centum*, (without the advantages and entertainments) which the Captain distributeth among the best deserving souldiers.

The Captains or other officers which are reformed (that is, dismissed from their service, for their age or otherwise) have their wonted pay continued.

The Quartermaster Generall hath 25. crowns a moneth, and each of his assistants 15.

The chief Chaplain hath 30.

The Auditor 30, and 18. for his three officers.

The Provost Marshall hath 25, and for every of his men (which must not exceed 12.) he hath 5 crowns.

The chief Chirurgeon hath 25.

In winter when the Cavallrie is in garrison, the souldiers are paid by the day, for the better keeping of their horses.

C

To

To the Generall 40. places are allowed as Generall, and 10 as Captain.

To the Lieutenant Generall 20, and 10 as Captain.

To the Commissarie Generall 10, and 10 as Captain.

To every Captain 10.

To the Lieutenant 6.

To the Cornet 4.

To the reformed officers 1½.

To the Auditor 6.

To the Quartermaster Generall 4.

To each of his assistants 2.

To the Provost Marshall 2, and 1 to each of his men.

To the chief Chaplain 5.

a *Picotine.*   Every place is worth 13. stuyvers (about 16. pence English) of these 13. stuyvers, 10 are paid for forrage, and 3. for service. Half of the said 13. stuyvers is paid to the souldiers in money, the other half in 16 pound of hay, three small measures of oats, and two bundles of straw, which are sufficient to keep a horse for a day.

At the end of the accounts, every souldier is abated half a reall (3 pence) upon every place.

The severall payes given by the States of the united Provinces at this day, being reduced to English money, are much about this proportion following.

To the Generall of horse 4 *per diem.*

To the Lieutenant Generall 2.

b *Or Commissarie Generall.*   To the b Sergeant Major 10.

To the Quartermaster Generall 6 8d.

To the Provost 5.

To the Carriage-master 3 4d.

To the Preacher 4.

To the chief Chirurgeon 4.

Note, that the Captain of horse mustereth 6 horse, the Lieutenant 4, the Cornet 3, for which they receive allowance extraordinarie.   To the Captains 8.

To the Lieutenant 5.

To the Cornets 4,

To the Corporalls 2 6d.

To the Trumpets 2 6d.

To the Quartermasters 2 6d.

To the Chirurgeons 2 6d.

To the souldiers Cuirassiers 2.

To the Harquebusiers 1 6d.

CHAP. XVIII.

Of supplying the Cavallrie with good horses.

FOr the reforming of the Cavallrie, there is moreover required a singular care, that the companies be supplied with good horses: wherefore it will be necessarie, that when the Cavallrie is retired from the field, the Captains make sale of such horses as be unfit for service, and buy better. When the companies be entered into garrison, the souldiers which are on foot must presently be remounted; that so, in the time of winter, they may at leisure fit their horses for service: for a *Equos assiduo labore confectis adimati.* Veg. lib. 2. cap. 14.   being onely remounted at the time of their going into the field, the a horses are not fitted for service, and being young and not used to the bridle, by any little toil they become unprofitable: besides, when a man is put (on the sudden) to buy such as he findeth, they prove not onely the worser, but the dearer. Moreover, those souldiers which want horses are of no service; and these are they (usually) which straggle disbanded, and do most mischief about the quarters. And because oftentimes there is not money assigned apart to remount the souldiers, it were good that among the companies there were a brother-hood or fellowship erected, (which the Spanish call *Platta*) which consisteth in making a cash, wherein the money which is gathered to that end, is kept; as followeth. First, the souldiers of every companie choose foure of their most judicious fellows, with consent of the captain. These, with the farrier of the companie, must view all the horses of their companie, prizing every one according to his value, and concealing it from the souldiers, to avoid disputes: and of this prizing they must keep a record, that so, if any horse happen to die, it may be known what is to be allowed; provided alwayes, that they go no higher then 50. crowns. To raise this cash, the Captain must give order that a crown be defalked out of every souldiers first pay, foure realls out of a third pay, and eight out of the contributions of a moneth: or else this proportion to be for the first beginning, and afterwards the moitie; or more or lesse as need shall require,

Every horse dying in service, or by mischance, without the souldiers fault, shall be made good to the souldier that lost him.

If

ordereth to every man his due proportion. The Trumpets muſt have leave of the chief Commander of the place to ſell the ſaid bootie, and the buyer is to give one of every twentie to the trumpeter, for his pains in the ſale : which money is to be divided among the trumpeters which were employed in the taking of that bootie; they having no other ſhare.

If one or more horſes were hurt or killed in the combat, or any ſouldiers chanced to be hurt in the ſaid action, thoſe horſes muſt be made good, and the ſouldiers are to be recompenſed, before the bootie be divided, at the diſcretion of the Chief.

If any ſouldiers horſe fall lame, after the troop be marched a good diſtance from the quarter, ſo as he be forced to return back, yet ſhall that ſouldier have his ſhare of the bootie, as if he had been preſent at the taking thereof.

Moreover, concerning the taking of priſoners, becauſe other authours are ſcant in this particular, it will not be amiſſe (for the better ſatisfaction of ſuch as are not acquainted with that language) to adde ſomething out of the States edict, as followeth.

Artic. 59.

Every ſouldier (of what condition ſoever he be) ſhall forthwith, and before evening, bring all ſuch of the enemie as are taken priſoners before him, which commandeth in the quarter; upon pain of looſing his priſoner, and being puniſhed with death.

60.

And if any ſhould take ſome eminent officer, or commander of the enemie priſoner, or other perſon of qualitie ; they ſhall be bound to preſent the ſame (or cauſe him to be preſented and delivered) immediately to the Lords the States Generall, or the Councel of State, receiving for them (as alſo for other priſoners which the ſaid States ſhall take to themſelves) ſome reaſonable recompence, according to the qualitie or abilitie of the ſaid priſoners; yet not exceeding the ſumme of 500. pounds, whereby the ſaid priſoner ſhall remain at the diſpoſing of the ſaid States : and they which took him, ought to have no further pretence to him.

61.

It ſhall not be lawfull for any man to cauſe a priſoner to be killed, or ſet at ranſom: nor (after ranſom be paid) to ſuffer him to depart, without leave of the Generall, or of him that commandeth in the quarter, on pain of being diſarmed, and baniſhed out of the provinces.

62.

And if any priſoner be found to walk about the leaguer or place of garriſon, without leave of the Generall or Commander in that quarter or garriſon ; the partie which had taken him ſhall forfeit his ſaid priſoner, to the profit of him who firſt ſhall apprehend the ſaid priſoner.

All lawfull booties are to be certified by the takers thereof, to the Commander of the quarter within three houres after their arrivall; and are to be regiſtred, and ſold in the open market, &c. upon pains of forfeiture, and of corporall puniſhment, &c.

CHAP. XVII.

Of the Souldiers pay.

THe means to have theſe and other good orders duly obſerved, is , (as is above ſaid) by giving to the ſouldiers their pay in competent meaſure and due time. The proportion which was obſerved on the King of Spains ſide, ſince the end of the late truce with the States of the united Provinces, is as followeth.

The Generall of horſe his pay or entertainment, is 500. crowns a moneth, beſides 86½ for his companie.

The Lieutenant Generall 200. and 86½ for his companie.

The Commiſſarie Generall 80. and the pay of a Captain of Harquebuſiers, when he hath a companie.

The Captains of lances and Cuiraſſiers 80. and 6½ for their page.

The Lieutenant of lances and Cuiraſſiers 25. and 6½ for a page.

The Cornets 15. and 6½ for a page.

The ſouldiers of lances and Cuiraſſiers have 6½ crowns a moneth.

The Captains of Harquebuſiers have 70. crowns a moneth, and 6. for a page.

The Lieutenant 25. and 6. for a page.

The ſouldiers have ſix crowns a moneth.

On the Spaniſh ſide they were wont to allow no Cornet to the Harquebuſiers (as is elſewhere ſhewed) and therefore no pay is here ſet down for him;but that courſe is ſince altered, and his pay is onely one twelfth part inferiour to the pay of a Cornet of Cuiraſſiers.

Beſides theſe ſtipends, there is given to every companie 10. *per centum*, (without the advantages and entertainments) which the Captain diſtributeth among the beſt deſerving ſouldiers.

The Captains or other officers which are reformed (that is, diſmiſſed from their ſervice, for their age or otherwiſe) have their wonted pay continued.

The Quartermaſter Generall hath 25. crowns a moneth, and each of his aſſiſtants 15.

The chief Chaplain hath 30.

The Auditor 30, and 18. for his three officers.

The Provoſt Marſhall hath 25, and for every of his men (which muſt not exceed 12.) he hath 5 crowns.

The chief Chirurgeon hath 25.

In winter when the Cavallrie is in garriſon, the ſouldiers are paid by the day, for the better keeping of their horſes.

C

To

To the Generall 40. places are allowed as Generall, and 10 as Captain.

To the Lieutenant Generall 20, and 10 as Captain.

To the Commiſſarie Generall 10, and 10 as Captain.

To every Captain 10.

To the Lieutenant 6.

To the Cornet 4.

To the reformed officers 1½.

To the Auditor 6.

To the Quartermaſter Generall 4.

To each of his aſſiſtants 2.

To the Provoſt Marſhall 2, and 1 to each of his men.

To the chief Chaplain 5.

a Picotin.

Every place is worth 13. ſtuyvers (about 16. pence Engliſh) of theſe 13. ſtuyvers, 10 are paid for forrage, and 3. for ſervice. Half of the ſaid 13. ſtuyvers is paid to the ſouldiers in money, the other half in 16 pound of hay, three ſmall meaſures of oats, and two bundles of ſtraw, which are ſufficient to keep a horſe for a day.

At the end of the accounts, every ſouldier is abated half a reall (3 pence) upon every place.

The ſeverall payes given by the States of the united Provinces at this day, being reduced to Engliſh money, are much about this proportion following.

To the Generall of horſe 4ˡ *per diem.*

To the Lieutenant Generall 2ˡ.

*b Or Commiſ-
ſarie Generall.*

To the ᵇ Sergeant Major 30ˢ.

To the Quartermaſter Generall 6ˢ 8ᵈ.

To the Provoſt 5ˢ.

To the Carriage-maſter 3ˢ 4ᵈ.

To the Preacher 4ˢ.

To the chief Chirurgeon 4ˢ.

To the Captains 8ˢ.

Note, that the Captain of horſe muſtereth 6 horſe, the Lieutenant 4, the Cornet 3, for which they receive allowance extraordinarie.

To the Lieutenant 5ˢ.

To the Cornets 4ˢ,

To the Corporalls 2ˢ 6ᵈ.

To the Trumpets 2ˢ 6ᵈ.

To the Quartermaſters 2ˢ 6ᵈ.

To the Chirurgeons 2ˢ 6ᵈ.

To the ſouldiers Cuiraſſiers 2ˢ.

To the Harquebuſiers 1ˢ 6ᵈ.

CHAP. XVIII.

Of ſupplying the Cavallrie with good horſes.

FOr the reforming of the Cavallrie, there is moreover required a ſingular care, that the companies be ſupplied with good horſes: wherefore it will be neceſſarie, that when the Cavallrie is retired from the field, the Captains make ſale of ſuch horſes as be unfit for ſervice, and buy better. When the companies be entered into garriſon, the ſouldiers which are on foot muſt preſently be remounted; that ſo, in the time of winter, they may at leiſure fit their horſes for ſervice: for being onely remounted at the time of their going into the field, the horſes are not fitted for ſervice, and being young and not uſed to the bridle, by any little toil they become unprofitable: beſides, when a man is put (on the ſudden) to buy ſuch as he findeth, they prove not onely the worſer, but the dearer. Moreover, thoſe ſouldiers which want horſes are of no ſervice; and theſe are they (uſually) which ſtraggle disbanded, and do moſt miſchief about the quarters. And becauſe oftentimes there is not money aſſigned apart to remount the ſouldiers, it were good that among the companies there were a brother-hood or fellowſhip erected, (which the Spaniſh call *Platta*) which conſiſteth in making a caſh, wherein the money which is gathered to that end, is kept; as followeth. Firſt, the ſouldiers of every companie chooſe foure of their moſt judicious fellows, with conſent of the captain. Theſe, with the farrier of the companie, muſt view all the horſes of their companie, prizing every one according to his value, and concealing it from the ſouldiers, to avoid diſputes: and of this prizing they muſt keep a record, that ſo, if any horſe happen to die, it may be known what is to be allowed; provided alwayes, that they go no higher then 50. crowns. To raiſe this caſh, the Captain muſt give order that a crown be defalked out of every ſouldiers firſt pay, foure realls out of a third pay, and eight out of the contributions of a moneth: or elſe this proportion to be for the firſt beginning, and afterwards the moitie; or more or leſſe as need ſhall require.

a Equos aſſiduo labore contunit adſmark. Veg. lib. 1. cap. 14.

Every horſe dying in ſervice, or by miſchance, without the ſouldiers fault, ſhall be made good to the ſouldier that loſt him.

If

suffer their children to eat any meat, but that which they could hit at an appointed distance, with a stone cast out of a sling : by which means they grew so expert at it, as that people are said to be the inventers of that weapon, and therein to have excelled all others. Every mean trade requireth exercise for the obtaining of it; how much more the art Military ? which is *rebus omnibus potior, per quam libertas retinetur, & dignitas Provincia propagatur, & conservatur imperium :* that is, *by which libertie is continued, the dignity of the Province is propagated, and the Empire preserved.* And this is confirmed by *Josephus (Exid. lib. 3.)* to be true, that not fortune, but the good orders of the Romanes in their *militia,* made them masters of the world : whose forces even in times of peace, and (as it were) to keep their hands in ure, were 32000 foot, 2400 horse; but upon occasions they could make 70000 or 80000 : and at a view taken of their own forces, and their allies in *Italy,* there were found 700000 foot, and 70000 horse.   *Augustus* maintained 23 legions, *Tyberius* 25. In *Galbaes* time the State maintained 31 legions: so that ordinarily in those and later times, there were (of legionarie and auxiliarie souldiers) maintained 372000. foot, and 37200. horse : whose ordinary pay (besides corn and apparell) at one *denarius* a day for the foot, and three for the horse (besides the increase of wages given to the officers) amounteth to five millions, five hundred sixteen thousand sixtie two pounds and ten shillings by the yeare; which is more (as S[r]. H. *Savile* observeth) then the great Turk at this day receiveth in two yeares towards all charges. Besides these , they maintained a guard of many thousands for the Prince, with double pay, and others for other employments ; and yet they never mutined for lack of pay. [g] *O viros summâ admiratione laudandos* (may be said of them , as *Vegetius* saith of the Lacedemonians) *qui eam præcipuè artem ediscere voluerunt , sine qua aliæ artes esse non possunt!* that is , *O men worthy to be praised with highest admiration , which would principally learn that art,* (speaking of the art militarie) *without which other arts cannot subsist!* But now , if we shall compare our times with these, must we not be forced to crie out with [h] *Lipsius, O pudor, O dedecus!*

The Low-countreys are (without all controversie) worthily styled the Academie of warre, where the art militarie (if any where) truly flourisheth; and yet, in comparison of the Romanes, the said *Lipsius* is constrained to say (who would not speak the worst of his own countrey) *Exercitium nobis neglectum, &c. Ubi campi doctores nostri sunt? ubi quotidiana meditationes armorum, &c. With us* (saith he) *exercise is neglected. Where are our teachers for the field? where are our daily practisings of arms?* Or whereas otherwise [i] no man professeth any art which he hath not learned, shall the militarie art be onely that which men suppose they can leap into, and be expert in, both at an instant ? *Tympanum sonuit &c. The drumme beats,* they run together, and enter their names with the Clerk of the band, something they change in their habit, and their gate; they swagger and drink; *ecce jam miles, behold* (saith he) *here is a souldier already,* Another complaineth after the like manner. [k] See (saith he) what our militia and militarie discipline is come to , and principally this so noble a part of it. (speaking of the horse) A clown is laden with arms, and mounted on horseback, that is enough for the Cavallrie.

Now if we should bring our trained bands (especially the horse) to the touchstone, and trie what alloy they be of, I fear we may ask (with *Lipsius*) *Hæc ridenda, an miseranda sunt?*

A principall defence and bulwark of the kingdome, consisteth in having the trained bands (horse and foot) well chosen, well armed, and well disciplined. But how this is generally in every part neglected is too shamefully apparent, Whether for want of good laws, or of good men to see them strictly executed, it is not for me to determine. Sure I am, there is great need of reformation. But my zeal transports me beyond my bounds, and I digresse from what I intended; therefore, for this matter, *hic terminus esto.*

[g] Virtus militaris præstat cæteris omnibus, Cicero pro Mar.
Nobilis res atque inprimis usitu, militaris est scientia, &c. Leo. Tact. cap. 10.
[h] De militia Rom. lib. 5.

[i] Omnes artes in meditatione consistunt. Athletæ, auriga, venator, propter exiguam mercedem, vel certè plebis favorem, quotidianâ meditatione artes suas aut servare, aut augere consuescunt. Militem (cujus est manibusservanda respublica) studiosius oportet scientiam dimicandi, usumq; rei bellica jugibus exercitiis custodire. Cui c.mingit non tantum gloriosa vi°toria, sed etiam amplior præda, quemque ad opes ac dignitates

ordo militia & imperatoris judicium consuevit evehere. Veg. lib. 1. cap. 24.   [k] Voyla que c' est de nostre milice et discipline militaire, et principalement de ceste partie, tant noble ; Un rustault chargé d' armes, et monté a cheval, c'est assez pour la Cavalrie, Walhausen. Discipline hodie non dicam languet apud nos, sed obiit : neque mala, sed nulla est. Lips. Politic. lib. 5. cap. 13.   Hodiernam militiam tristi oculo intueor; pudendam lugendamque nobis, hosti ridendam aut spernendam. Ibid. cap. 8.

CHAP. XXVII.

Of Exercising in particular.

Of managing of the horse and arms.

THe Cavallrie being to be exercised , must be instructed how to manage their horse and their arms.

Concerning the horse (presupposing him to be of sufficient stature and strength, nimble of joynts , and sure of foot, &c.) he must (of necessitie) be made fit for service, so as you may have him ready at command to pace, trot, gallop, or run in full career; also to advance, stop, retire, and turn readily to either hand, and all with alacritie and obedience. Now, to bring him to this readie turning, he is to be ridden the ring, and figure 8, first in a great compasse, and so in a lesse by degrees, first upon his pace, then on the trot, and so to the gallop and career. These things he may be taught by using the hand, leg, and voice. For the hand (observing not to move the arm,

but

but onely the wrist) if you would have him to face to the left, a little motion of the little finger on that rein, and a touch of the left leg (without using the spurre) doth it : if to face (or turn) to the left about, a harder, &c. If you would have him to trot, you are to move both your legs a little forward; for the gallop, to move them more forward; and for the career to yerk them most forward, and to move the bodie a little forward with it. After every motion performed, it were good to keep him a while in that motion, as when you bid him stand, to stand a while, &c. Also it were not amisse, after every thing well done, to give him some bread or grasse as a reward. For the voice, you may use the words, Advance, hold, turn, or the like; but because the voice cannot always be heard, it were good to use him chiefly to the motions of the hand and leg. It will also be very usefull to teach him to go sidewayes : this he may be brought unto by laying his provender somewhat farre from him in the manger, and keeping him from turning his head towards it. He must also be used to the smell of gunpowder, the sight of fire and armour, and the bearing of shot, drummes and trumpets, &c, but by degrees and with discretion. When he is at his oats (at a good distance from him) a little powder may be fired, and so nearer to him by degrees. So may a pistoll be fired some distance off, and so nearer : in like manner a drum or trumpet may be used. The groom may sometime dresse him in armour, and he may be used (now and then) to eat his oats from the drum head. It will be very usefull sometime to cause a musketier to stand at a convenient distance, and both of you to give fire upon each other, and thereupon to ride up close to him : also to ride him against a compleat armour, so set upon a stake, that he may overthrow it, and trample it under his feet: that so (and by such other means) your horse (finding that he receiveth no hurt) may become bold to approch any object. He may also be used to mountanous and uneven wayes, and be exercised to leap, swim, and the like. But for further directions for the art of riding and managing the horse, I referre the reader to [a] them which have written of horsemanship *ex professo*, whose books are every where obvious.

a Besides many of our own writers; *Pierre de la Noüe* in his Cavallerie Françoise et Italienne. also Instruction du Roy (de France) en l'exercice de monter a Cheval, par Antoyne de Pluvinel, lately published, and divers others.

CHAP. XXVIII.

Of managing arms, extending to postures and motions.

Of exercising the lance.

HOwsoever the use of the lance be now left off in the Low-countreys, either for the reasons alledged chap. 23, or by reason of the discommoditie of the countrey (for the lance is of no use but in a spacious, hard, and uneven ground) yet will it not be altogether impertinent to shew the manner of exercising the same, seeing that many have taken pains to revive unto us the knowledge of those arms which sometime were in use among the Grecians, Romanes, and other nations, which have been for many ages totally abolished.

The manner of carrying the lance, is either advanced, or couched; that is, when it is carried so abased, as the enemie can hardly discover it untill he feel the shock.

The charging of the lance is twofold, either by the right, or left.

The right is, when it is presented or charged along by the right side of the horse.

The left is, when it is born acrosse the neck of the horse, by the left eare.

The first is the manner used by the Turks and Hungarians, and by some preferred before the other. One reason which they give for it, is, because that in charging by the left, the Lancier must incline his bodie to the left, and so sitteth the lesse sure in his saddle.

Basta would have the second way to be best. Howsoever, all agree that a Lancier must ever strive to gain the left side of his enemie, and charge him on the left.

Now there be three wayes of charging;

1 By carrying the lance sloaped upwards.

2 By charging it levell, in a straight line.

3 By charging it sloaping, or inclining downwards.

The first is, if against Cavallrie, to take the sight of the enemie with the point of the lance; or, if against foot, the head or neck of either pike or musketier.

The second is, by charging a horse-man about the middle, (to bear him out of the saddle) or on the breast of the foot.

The third serveth to pierce the breast of the enemies horse, or a kneeling musketier, or pike charging at the foot against horse.

These three severall wayes must be diligently practised, and require much dexteritie: to which end a stake is to be set up, having an arm (as it were) stretched out from it, and thereunto a white (either of paper or linen) fastned, at severall heights, which the Lancier must exercise himself to hit in full career ; also to take up a glove (or the like from the ground with the point of his lance, &c. All which is here shown *figure. 2. part. 1. chap.* 28. In his charging of the enemie, he begins upon his pace or trot, [b] then falls into a gallop, but must not begin his career untill he be

a L. Lips. *Homocquatoriæ*. Item de Milit. Rom. N Machiavelli. G. du Bellay. C. Bingham upon Æliau. Sir Cl. Edmonds on Cæs. Com. Sir Hen. Savile, &c.

b Monsieur de La Noüe, blameth the French for their errour in this point. *De 100 pas ils commencent à galloper, et de 100 à courir à toute bride, qui est faire erreur, n'estant besoin de prendre tant d'espace. Discours 18.*

within

suffer their children to eat any meat, but that which they could hit at an appointed distance, with a stone cast out of a sling : by which means they grew so expert at it, as that people are said to be the inventers of that weapon, and therein to have excelled all others. Every mean trade requireth exercise for the obtaining of it; how much more the art Military ? which is *rebus omnibus potior, per quam libertas retinetur, & dignitas Provinciæ propagatur, & conservatur imperium :* that is, *by which libertie is continued, the dignity of the Province is propagated, and the Empire preserved.* And this is confirmed by *Josephus* (*Exid. lib. 3.*) to be true, that not fortune, but the good orders of the Romanes in their *militia,* made them masters of the world : whose forces even in times of peace, and (as it were) to keep their hands in ure, were 32000 foot, 2400 horse; but upon occasions they could make 70000 or 80000 : and at a view taken of their own forces, and their allies in *Italy,* there were found 700000 foot, and 70000 horse. *Augustus* maintained 23 legions, *Tyberius* 25. In *Galbaes* time the State maintained 31 legions : so that ordinarily in those and later times, there were (of legionarie and auxiliarie souldiers) maintained 372000. foot, and 37200. horse : whose ordinary pay (besides corn and apparell) at one *denarius* a day for the foot, and three for the horse (besides the increase of wages given to the officers) amounteth to five millions, five hundred sixteen thousand sixtie two pounds and ten shillings by the yeare: which is more (as S[r]. H. *Savile* observeth) then the great Turk at this day receiveth in two yeares towards all charges. Besides these, they maintained a guard of many thousands for the Prince, with double pay, and others for other employments; and yet they never mutined for lack of pay. [g] *O viros summâ admiratione laudandos* (may be said of them, as *Vegetius* saith of the Lacedemonians) *qui eam præcipuè artem ediscere voluerunt, sine qua aliæ artes esse non possunt!* that is, O men *worthy to be praised with highest admiration, which would principally learn that art,* (speaking of the art militarie) *without which other arts cannot subsist!* But now, if we shall compare our times with these, must we not be forced to crie out with [h] *Lipsius, O pudor, O dedecus!*

The Low-countreys are (without all controversie) worthily styled the Academie of warre, where the art militarie (if any where) truly flourisheth; and yet, in comparison of the Romanes, the said *Lipsius* is constrained to say (who would not speak the worst of his own countrey) *Exercitium nobis neglectum, &c. Ubi campi doctores nostri sunt? ubi quotidianæ meditationes armorum, &c. With us* (saith he) *exercise is neglected. Where are our teachers for the field? where are our daily practisings of arms?* Or whereas otherwise [i] no man professeth any art which he hath not learned, shall the militarie art be onely that which men suppose they can leap into, and be expert in, both at an instant ? *Tympanum sonuit &c. The drumme beats,* they run together, and enter their names with the Clerk of the band, something they change in their habit, and their gate; they swagger and drink; *ecce jam miles, behold* (saith he) *here is a souldier already.* Another complaineth after the like manner. [k] See (saith he) what our militia and militarie discipline is come to, and principally this so noble a part of it. (speaking of the horse) A clown is laden with arms, and mounted on horseback, that is enough for the Cavallrie.

Now if we should bring our trained bands (especially the horse) to the touchstone, and trie what alloy they be of, I fear we may ask (with *Lipsius*) *Hæc ridenda, an miseranda sunt?*

A principall defence and bulwark of the kingdome, consisteth in having the trained bands (horse and foot) well chosen, well armed, and well disciplined. But how this is generally in every part neglected is too shamefully apparent, Whether for want of good laws, or of good men to see them strictly executed, it is not for me to determine. Sure I am, there is great need of reformation. But my zeal transports me beyond my bounds, and I digresse from what I Intended; therefore, for this matter, *hic terminus esto.*

ordo militiæ & imperatoriæ judicium consuevit evehere. Veg. lib. 2. cap. 24.   k Voyla que c' est de nostre milice et discipline militaire, et principalement de ceste partie, tant noble ; Un rustault chargé d' armes, et monté a cheval, c'est assez pour la Cavallrie. *Walhausen.* *Disciplina hodie non dicam languet apud nos, sed obiit: neque mala, sed nulla est.* Lipsi Politic. lib. 5. cap. 13.   Hodiernam militiam tristi oculo intueor y pudendam lugendâmque nobis, hosti ridendam aut spernendam. Ibid. cap. 8.

g *Virtus militaris præstit cæteris omnibus.* Cicero pro Mar. *Nobilis res atqua inprimis utilis, militaris est scientia, &c.* Leo. Tact. cap. 20.
h De militia Rom. lib. 5.

i *Omnes artes in meditatione consistunt. Athletæ, auriga, venator, propter exiguam mercedem, vel certè plebus eventem, quotidianâ meditatione artes suas aut servare, aut augere consuescunt. Militem (cujus est membra servanda respublicæ) studiosius oportet scientiam dimicandi, usumq; rei bellica jugibus exercitiis custodire. Cui eveningit non tantùm gloriosa victoria, sed etjam amplior præda, quæmque ad opes ac dignitates*

CHAP. XXVII.

Of Exercising in particular.

Of managing of the horse and arms.

THe Cavallrie being to be exercised, must be instructed how to manage their horse and their arms.

Concerning the horse (presupposing him to be of sufficient stature and strength, nimble of joynts, and sure of foot, &c.) he must (of necessitie) be made fit for service; so as you may have him ready at command to pace, trot, gallop, or run in full career; also to advance, stop, retire, and turn readily to either hand, and all with alacritie and obedience. Now, to bring him to this readie turning, he is to be ridden the ring, and figure 8, first In a great compasse, and so in a lesse by degrees, first upon his pace, then on the trot, and so to the gallop and career. These things he may be taught by using the hand, leg, and voice. For the hand (observing not to move the arm,

but

but onely the wrist) if you would have him to face to the left, a little motion of the little finger on that rein, and a touch of the left leg (without using the spurre) doth it : if to face (or turn) to the left about, a harder, &c. If you would have him to trot, you are to move both your legs a little forward; for the gallop , to move them more forward; and for the career to yerk them most forward , and to move the bodie a little forward with it. After every motion performed, it were good to keep him a while in that motion, as when you bid him stand, to stand a while, &c. Also it were not amisse, after every thing well done, to give him some bread or grasse as a reward. For the voice, you may use the words, Advance, hold, turn, or the like; but because the voice cannot alwayes be heard, it were good to use him chiefly to the motions of the hand and leg. It will also be very usefull to teach him to go sidewayes : this he may be brought unto by laying his provender somewhat farre from him in the manger , and keeping him from turning his head towards it. He must also be used to the smell of gunpowder, the sight of fire and armour, and the hearing of shot, drummes and trumpets, &c. but by degrees and with discretion. When he is at his oats (at a good distance from him) a little powder may be fired, and so nearer to him by degrees. So may a pistoll be fired some distance off, and so nearer : in like manner a drum or trumpet may be used. The groom may sometime dresse him in armour , and he may be used (now and then) to eat his oats from the drum head. It will be very usefull sometime to cause a musketier to stand at a convenient distance, and both of you to give fire upon each other , and thereupon to ride up close to him : also to ride him against a compleat armour , so set upon a stake, that he may overthrow it, and trample it under his feet: that so (and by such other means) your horse (finding that he receiveth no hurt) may become bold to approch any object. He may also be used to mountanous and uneven wayes, and be exercised to leap, swim, and the like. But for further directions for the art of riding and managing the horse, I referre the reader to [a] them which have written of horsemanship *ex professo*, whose books are every where obvious.

a Besides many of our own writers, *Pierre de la Noüe* in his *Cavallerie Françoise et Italienne.* also *Instruction du Roy* (de France) en l'exercice de monter a Cheval, par Antoyne de Pluvinel. lately published, and divers others.

CHAP. XXVIII.

Of managing arms, extending to postures and motions.

Of exercising the lance.

HOwsoever the use of the lance be now left off in the Low-countreys, either for the reasons alledged chap. 23, or by reason of the discommoditie of the countrey (for the lance is of no use but in a spacious, hard, and uneven ground) yet will it not be altogether impertinent to shew the manner of exercising the same, seeing that [a] many have taken pains to revive unto us the knowledge of those arms which sometime were in use among the Grecians, Romanes, and other nations, which have been for many ages totally abolished.

a I. Lips. *Poliorceumaticb. from de Milit. Rom.* N. Machiavell. G. du Bellay. C. Bingham *upon Ælian.* Sir Cl. Edmonds *on Cæs. Com.* Sir Hen. Savile, &c.

The manner of carrying the lance, is either advanced, or couched; that is, when it is carried so abased, as the enemie can hardly discover it untill he feel the shock.

The charging of the lance is twofold, either by the right, or left,

The right is, when it is presented or charged along by the right side of the horse.

The left is, when it is borne acrosse the neck of the horse; by the left eare.

The first is the manner used by the Turks and Hungarians , and by some preferred before the other. One reason which they give for it, is, because that in charging by the left, the Lancier must incline his bodie to the left, and so sitteth the lesse sure in his saddle.

Basta would have the second way to be best. Howsoever , all agree that a Lancier must ever strive to gain the left side of his enemie, and charge him on the left.

Now there be three wayes of charging;

1 By carrying the lance sloaped upwards.

2 By charging it levell, in a straight line.

3 By charging it sloaping, or inclining downwards.

The first is, if against Cavallrie , to take the sight of the enemie with the point of the lance; or, if against foot, the head or neck of either pike or musketier.

The second is, by charging a horse-man about the middle , (to bear him out of the saddle) or on the breast of the foot.

The third serveth to pierce the breast of the enemies horse , or a kneeling musketier, or pike charging at the foot against horse.

These three severall wayes must be diligently practised, and require much dexteritie: to which end a stake is to be set up, having an arm (as it were) stretched out from it; and thereunto a white (either of paper or linen) fastned , at severall heights, which the Lancier must exercise himself to hit in full career ; also to take up a glove (or the like from the ground with the point of his lance, &c. All which is here shown *figure* 2. *part*. 1. *chap*. 28. In his charging of the enemie, he begins upon his pace or trot, [b] then falls into a gallop, but must not begin his career untill he be

b Monsieur de la Noüe, blameth the French for their errour in this point. *De 200 par ils commencent à galloper , et de 100 à courir à toute bride, qui est faire errenr, n'estant besoin de prendre tant d'espace. Discours 18.*

within

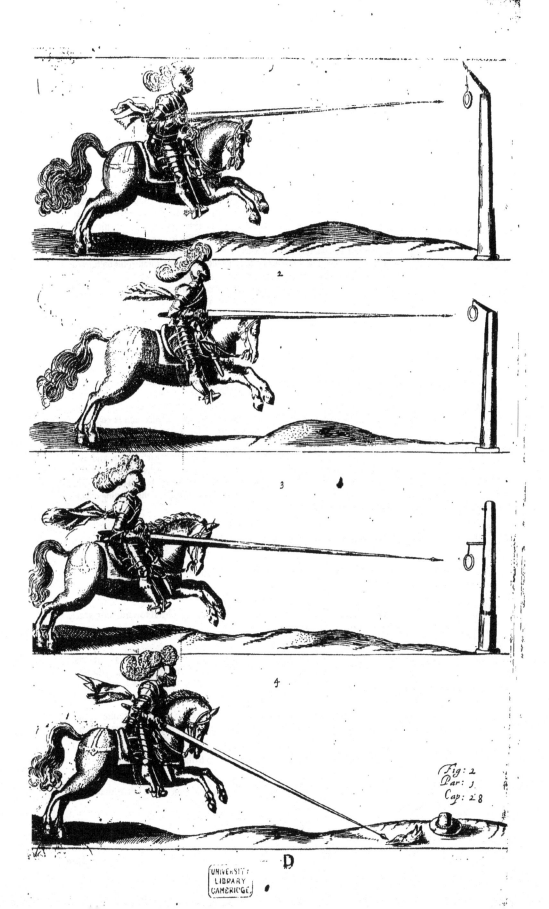

2

3

4

Fig: 2
Par: 1
Cap: 28

D

within some 60. paces of his enemie ; presenting his lance (from the advance) at the half of that distance, and charging it for the shock as occasion serveth. Against an armed Lancier, the best way of charging is judged to be, not after the two first wayes, but by the third, that is, at the breast of the horse, and that towards the left side of him, where his heart and vitals are; and for this, the charging by the right is held best.

Having given his charge with the lance, so as it becometh unusefull to him, he must betake himself to his pistoll, in the use whereof he is to be very skilfull. His last refuge is his sword, which he must also be well practised in. Of both which weapons shall be spoken in the next chapter.

CHAP. XXIX.
Of exercising the Cuirassier.

ALthough it be supposed and expected that no horse-man will presume to mount his horse to repair to his Cornet, before his pistols, harquebuse, or carabine be spanned, primed, and laden : his cases furnished with cartouches and all other equipage belonging to himself, his horse, and arms, made fix and in a readinesse : yet in case a Cuirassier upon service should (though unlikely) spend both his pistols, and the six cartouches wherewith his cases were filled, so that he must resort to his flask; and my present task being to teach the untutored Cuirassier his postures; it will not be impertinent here to set them down in the largest manner.

Now because these things are to be performed on horseback, it will not be unnecessary (though mounting on horseback be accounted no posture, but a preparative to exercise or service) first to shew how he is to mount(which with the rest of the postures is done in *Figure* 3. *Part* 1. *Chap.* 29.) and for this, the word of command is,

1. *To Horse.*

a The horse-man being to mount, must be carefull that his horse be very well girt. Such was the admirable industrie of the Romanes, as that all their horse-men were continually practised to mount on wooden horses, and that on either sides first unarmed, afterwards compleatly armed, also with drawn swords or lances in their hands, without the help of stirrops (which were not known in those times.) Hoc enim continua meditatione faciebant, scilicet ut in tumultu prælii sine more ascenderent, qui tam studiose exercebantur in pace. Veg. lib. 1. cap. 18.

Both reins hanging in a loose position over the horse neck, and upon the pummel of the saddle, the horseman is, First, to take the ends of the reins above the button in his right hand, and with the thumbe and two first fingers of that hand, to draw them to an even length. Then putting the little finger of his left hand betwixt both reins under the button, with the other three fingers of the same hand on the further rein, and the thumbe on the near side of the button, to grasp both reins, that so (before he endeavour to mount) he may have his horse head in ballance and at command: Then grasping the pummel of the saddle with his left hand, and standing with his full body close to the horse-side, and just between the bolster and cantle of the saddle (alwayes on the near side of the horse) with the help of his right hand he shall put the left foot into the left stirrop, and with his right hand taking fast hold on the highest part of the cantle behinde, he shall (with the help of both hands) gently yet strongly, and in a right-up posture, without inclining his body to either hand) raise himself untill he may stand perpendicular upon his left foot, and then putting over his right legge, place himself in the saddle.

2. *Uncap your pistols.*
With the right hand he is to turn down the caps of the pistol-cases.

3. *Draw your pistol.*
He is to draw the pistol out of the case with the right hand, (and alwayes the left pistol first) and to mount the muzzle of it, as in *posture* 15.

4. *Order your pistol.*
He is to sink the pistol into his bridle-hand, and to remove his right hand towards the muzzel, and then to rest the but end upon his thigh.

5. *Span your pistol.*
He is to sink the pistol into his bridle hand, and taking the key (or spanner) into his right hand, to put it upon the axletree, and to winde about the wheel till it stick : and then to return the spanner to his place, being usually fastened to the side of the case.

6. *Prime.*
Holding the pistol in the bridle-hand (as before) he is to take his priming box into his right hand, and (pressing the spring with his fore-finger to open the box) to put powder into the pan.

7. *Shut your pan.*
He is to presse in the pan-pin with his right thumbe, and so to shut the pan.

8. *Cast about your pistol.*
With the bridle-hand he is to cast about the pistol, and to hold it on the left side, with the muzzel upward.

9. *Gage your flasque.*
He is to take the flasque into the right hand, and with his forefinger to pull back the spring, and turning the mouth of the flasque downward, to let go the spring.

10. *Lade your pistol.*

Having gaged his flasque (as in the former posture) he is to presse down the spring, which openeth the flasque, with his forefinger, and so to lade his pistol.

11. *Draw your rammer.*

He is to draw his rammer with the right hand turned, and to hold it with the head downward.

12. *Lade with bullet, and ramme home.*

Holding the rammer-head in his right hand (as before) he is to take the bullet out of his mouth, or out of the bulletbag at the pistolcase, being in fight, with the thumbe and forefinger, and to put it into the muzzel of the pistol, and the rammer immediately after it, and so to ramme home.

13. *Return your rammer.*

He is to draw forth his rammer with the right hand turned, and to return it to its place.

14. *Pull down your cock.*

With the bridle-hand he is to bring the pistol towards his right side; and placing the but end upon his thigh, to pull down the cock.

15. *Recover your pistol.*

He is to take the pistol into his right hand, mounting the muzzel.

16. *Present and give fire.*

Having the pistol in his right hand (as in posture 15.) with his forefinger upon the tricker, he is to incline the muzzel (with a fixed eye) towards his mark; not suddenly, but by degrees, (quicker or slower according to the pace he rideth) and that not directly forward toward the horse head, but towards the right; turning his right hand so as the lock of the pistol may be upward : and having gotten his mark, he is to draw the tricker, and give fire.

17. *Return your pistol.*

He is to return his pistol into the case, and then to draw his other pistol (as occasion may serve) and to do as before.

Now concerning the snap-hane pistol, those postures wherein it differeth from the fire-lock pistol are these, (as in figure)

18. *Bend your cock.*

Holding the pistol in the bridle-hand (as before hath been shewed) with the right hand he is to bend the cock.

19. *Guard your cock.*

With the right hand he is to pull down the back-lock, so to secure the cock from going off.

20. *Order your hammer.*

With the right hand he is to draw down the hammer upon the pan.

21. *Free your cock.*

With the right thumbe he is to thrust back the back-lock, and so to give the cock liberty.

But the more compendious way of lading, for the gaining of time (which in the instant of skirmish is chiefly to be regarded) is by using cartouches. Now, the cartouch is to be made of white paper, cut out of convenient breadth and length, and rolled upon a stick, (or the rammer, if it be not too little) fit (according to the bore of the barrell) to contain a due quantity of powder, and the bullet. The proportion of powder usually required is half the weight of the bullet; but that is held too much by such as can judge. Having moulded the paper, the one end of it is to be turned in, (to keep in the powder)and the due charge of powder to be put into it at the other end; which powder is to be closed in by tying a little thred about the paper : then the bullet is to be put in, and that also tied in with a little thred. When the Cuirassier is to use his cartouch, he must bite off the paper at the head of it, and so put it into the barrell of his pistol, with the bullet upward, and then ramme it home. By [b] this means he shall much expedite the lading of his pistol. The Cuirassier being become ready in his postures, his next and chiefest study is, to be an exact marks-man. And to this end he must frequently be practised at some * marks, to be set up at some tree or stake, of severall heights. Now because the Cuirassier is armed pistol-proof he must not give fire but at a very near distance, being carefull to bestow his bullets so, as they may take effect. The principall place of advantage to aim at, is the lower part of the belly of the adverse Cuirassier, also his arm-pits, or his neck. Some would not have a Cuirassier to give * fire, until he have placed his pistol under his enemies armour, or on some unarmed parts. If he fail of an opportunity to hurt the man, he may aim at the breast of the horse, or his head, as he shall see occasion. He usually giveth his

[b] For the more speedy lading of the pistol, and avoiding the trouble of carrying either flasque or touch-box, there is a late invented fashion of spanner or key, (which I have represented in figure 1.) which contains six charges of powder (at the least) and priming powder sufficient for those charges, and for the cartouches wherewith the pistol cases be furnished: which the Cuirassier will find to be of very good use, when he is used thereunto.

c The Romanes exercised their souldiers at severall heights at stakes set up in *Campo Martio: Ad palum quoque vel sudes juniors exerceri percommodum est, cum latera, vel pedes, aut caput petere punctim caecimque condiscant.* Veg. lib. 2, cap. 23. But their manner of fighting with their swords was not caesim, but all upon the thrust or point; because that manner sooner pierced the mentls, and laid not open the body in fetching of a blow. *Ibid. lib. 1. cap. 12.*
* *La pistole ne fait quasi nul effect, si elle n'est tirée de trois pas, Monsieur de la Nove, discours* 19 , ° Les Reistres bien instructs ne deschargent point leurs pistolles qu'en heurtant; qu'ils addressent touisours aux cuisses ou aux visages. *Ibid.*

f As is shewed in the postures 22.

charge upon the trot, and seldome galloppeth, unlesse it be in pursuit of a flying enemie, or such like occasion. Having spent both his pistols, and wanting time to lade again, his next refuge is his sword; whereof the best manner of using is to place the pummell of it upon his right [f] thigh, and so with his right hand to direct or raise the point to his mark, higher or lower as occasion serveth; either at the belly of the adverse horse-man (about the pummel of the saddle) or at his arm-pits, or his throat; where if it pierce not (as it is very like it will not fail, by slipping under the casque) yet meeting with a stay in that part of the body where a man is very weak, and having a sword of a very stiff blade, as aforesaid, it will doubtlesse unhorse him. Being past his enemie, he is to make a back-blow at him, aiming to cut the buckle of his pouldron, whereby he disarmeth one of his arms, &c. *Basta* highly commendeth the aiming at the enemies sight, and so (by raising the vizures of his casque with the point of the sword) to run him into the head. But this seemeth not so likely to take effect as that of aiming at the throat; and sometimes (as some casques are made) it would be of no use.

In these and the like exercises the Cuirassier is frequently and diligently to practise himself at some mark; which will render him fit for service when need shall require.

Some authors (for the disposing of the Cuirassiers for fight) hold that they ought to be ordered in grosse bodies, that so [s] by their solidity and weight, they may entertain and sustain the shock of the enemie. They are also fit for troops of reserve, to give courage to the other Cavallrie, and to give them opportunity to re-assemble themselves behind them, &c.

CHAP. XXX.

Of exercising the Harquebusier and Carabine.

ALthough there be some difference between the Harquebusier and the Carabine, in regard of their horse, their arming, and their piece, (howsoever most authors take them for one and the same) yet in regard the harquebuse differeth nothing from the carabine in length, but onely in the bore, their manner of using their severall pieces is one and the same; and so one instruction may serve for both.

In march, he is either to carry his carabine hanging at his belt by the right side, (as is shewed chap. 24.) or else to order it upon his right thigh, as the Cuirassier, in *posture* 4.

In fight he is to strive to gain the left side of his enemy, (contrary to the Cuirassier) because that in presenting he is to rest his carabine on his bridle-hand, placing the but end on the right side of his breast, near his shoulder.

He must be taught to use his carabine with all exactnesse and dexterity, and to be an exquisite marks-man. For the manner of handling of the harquebuse or carabine, the directions for the pistol, in the foregoing chapter, *mutatis mutandis,* may serve for sufficient instruction. Yet in regard the carabines with us are for the most part snap-hanes, and so something differing from the fire-lock, I will set down the order of handling it, in the words of command: holding it need lesse here to dilate them.

Postures for the snap-hane carabine.

1 Order your carabine.	11 Shorten your rammer.
2 Sink your carabine into your bridle-hand.	12 Lade with bullet, and ramme home.
3 Bend your cock.	13 Withdraw your rammer.
4 Guard your cock.	14 Shorten your rammer.
5 Prime.	15 Return your rammer.
6 Shut your pan.	16 Recover your carabine.
7 Cast about your carabine.	17 Order your hammer.
8 Gage your flasque.	18 Free your cock.
9 Lade your carabine.	19 Present.
10 Draw your rammer.	20 Give fire.

For the use of his sword, he is to demean himself as the Cuirassier.

CHAP. XXXI.

Of exercising the Dragon.

THe Dragon was invented for speciall services to assist the Cavallrie as Infantery, considering there be many exploits which cannot be effected by the Cavallrie alone.

The musketier must exercise himself to give fire on horseback, as the Harquebusier. Being come to guard a passage, or to do any other the like service, they are to alight, and to demean themselves as Infantery. Whereof it shall be needlesse here to enlarge, seeing we have books in such abundance upon that subject, as they are able rather to [a] distract, then instruct the reader, and in my opinion, had need of an *Index expurgatorius.*

Being so alighted to do their service (as abovesaid) every of them is to cast his bridle over the
neck

neck of his side-mans horse, in the same order as they marched: keeping them so together, by the help of such as are thereunto especially appointed.

CHAP. XXXII.
Of exercising the Cavallrie in their motions.

HAving shewed how every horse-man is to be exercised in the managing of his horse, as also in the use of his particular arms; it followeth now that he be taught how to demean himself, being joyned in a body.

And here, before we enter into the motions, it were fit to explain the terms of art therein used, and to shew what is meant by a file, a rank, half files, and half ranks; the front, flanks, and rear, and the like. But (for brevitie sake) I passe them over, referring the reader to the books of Infanterie.

To exercise the horse, they are to be drawn up into a body, not by ranks, but by files; and those of five deep, as most affirm; or of six, as others would have it: and that because the number of five is not divisible by two, and so in doubling of ranks, or half files, or the like, there is always an odde rank. Some would have them (especially the harquebusiers) to be eight in file, taking the troop to consist of 64. Being put in *Battalia*, that is, ordered into a square body, and silence strictly commanded; the first thing to be taught them, is distance. And herein authors disagree. Some make close order to be two paces; open order, foure paces; and so for double, triple, and quadruple distance proportionable. Others make but two kinds of distances; close order, which is three foot; and open order, which is six foot. But this must be understood *cum grano salis*, (as the Civilians speak:) for here we must observe a difference between the manner of taking the distance of the Cavallrie, and that of the Infantery : for in the foot, the distance is taken from the centre of the souldiers body, which here cannot be so understood, but onely of the space of ground between horse and horse.

Monsieur *de Praissac* is more plain, who would have the distance between rank and rank (both for the length of the horse, as also for the space between horse and horse) to be six paces, and one pace between file and file. Yet, if we take every pace for five foot (as that is the usuall dimention) by this rule they should be at a very large distance.

In my opinion, the Cavallrie being to be exercised in their motions, should be at their distance of six foot, or open order (taking it as hath been shewed) [b] standing right in their ranks and files.

[c] Now the motions are of foure kinds; 1. Facings. 2. Doublings. 3. Countermarches. 4. Wheelings.

The use of facings is to make the company perfect, to be suddenly prepared for a charge on either flank or the rear.

Doubling of ranks, or doubling by half files, or bringers up, is used upon occasion of strengthening the front.

Doubling of files, or doubling by half ranks, serveth to strengthen the flanks.

Countermarches serve, either to reduce the file-leaders into the place of the bringers up; and so to have the best men ready to receive the charge of an enemy in the rear; or to bring one flank into the place of the other: or front, and rear, or either flank into the middle of the body.

The use of wheelings, is to bring the front (which is alwayes supposed to consist of the ablest men) to be ready to receive the charge of the enemy on either flank or rear.

These motions (for the more easie apprehension of the untutored souldier) are represented in figures, by a company of harquebusiers of 64 men. And therein the file-leaders and bringers up are distinguished by a differing letter, as followeth.

[a] The Grecians and Romanes had the same order of exercise, and that in the same words which we retain to this day. A File, the Romanes called *Versus*, and *Decuria:* A Rank, *Jugum:* A File-leader, *Decanus*, because their *Decuria* (or File) used to consist of ten among the foot, with some 16. A bringer up,*Tergiductor:* A Leader (being every odde man in the file) *Prostes:* A follower (which is every even number)*Subiles:* A side-man,*Astes:* Their distances were the same with us. Their two cubits (every cubit being a foot and an half of our measure) agreed with our three foot. Their four cubits our 6 foot: and so increasing upon occasion. They ordered their horse-troops at six foot distance between file and file in march, and three foot in fight.
[b] *Omnes milites incedendi ordinem servent,*Veg. 1.9. *Ut aequali legitimoque spatio milites distet à milite;* *nec ultrà quàm expedit aut conglobent agmen aut laxint.* Ibid. cap. 16.
[c] In all the motions we also retain the same words of command which they used. Facing, they called *declinatio;* to the right hand, *ad hastam;* to the left, *ad scutum.* Facing about, *mutinatio.* Doubling, by ranks and files, *Duplicandi duo genera, per juga & versus.* Their countermarches the same which we use, *Evolutio Chorica, Macedonica, Laconica, per decurias & juga.* Wheelings the same with us, *Conversio ad hastam vel scutum. Reversio est conversionis restitutio. Inflexio,* wheeling about, &c.

The

The form of the first standing.
To face them to the right, is done by commanding

Front.

A A A A A A A A

a a a a a a a a
a a a a a a a a
a a a a a a a a
a a a a a a a a
a a a a a a a a
a a a a a a a a

Left flank.   *Right flank.*

a a a a a a a a

Rear.

To the right hand.

Which is done by turning (all at one and the same time) to the right hand. Thus the front is where the right flank was.

To reduce them to their first form, the word of command is, *As you were.*

Which they perform by turning to the left hand. From thence, to face them to the left, you command

---

To the left hand.

Which is performed by turning towards the left. From hence they are to be reduced by commanding, *As you were.* Which they do by turning to the right.

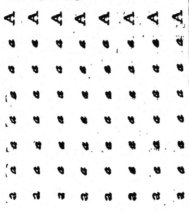

Now, to face them to the rear, though it be proper first to do it by the right hand, yet for the more ready way, I would say,

---

To the left hand about.

Which is done by turning towards the left hand, untill their faces front to that place which was before the rear.

To reduce them to their first form (as that must be observed) the word is,
To the right hand about, as you were.

Ranks, to the right double.	*Ranks, to the left double.*
The use hereof hath been shewed before. Every other rank, that is, every even number passeth into the odde, upon the right hand of his leader. The second rank into the first, and so successively.	The difference of this motion from the former, is nothing, but that here they which double do it to the left hand of their leaders, which before they did to their right hands, as the figure maketh it plain.

1 A a A a A a A a A a A a A a A a Aa	1 a A a A a A a A a A a A a A a A a A
2	2 . . . .
3 a a a a a a a a a a a a a a a a	3 a a a a a a a a a a a a a a a a
4	4 . . . .
5 a a a a a a a a a a a a a a a a	5 a a a a a a a a a a a a a a a a
6	6 . . . .
7 a a a a a a a a a a a a a a a a	7 a a a a a a a a a a a a a a a a
8	8 . . . .

To reduce them, the word is, *Ranks, as you were,* Which is best done, by causing those ranks which doubled to stand, and those which stood to advance.	This done, they must be reduced by commanding *Ranks, as you were.*

Files to the right double.	*Files to the left double.*
To do this, the second file passeth into the first (every man behind his sideman) accounting from the right hand: the fourth into the third, and so the rest: which must be done throughout the company at one instant, all together. But because the first rank of the company is as the edge, and the files are for the most part appointed but five deep, there seemeth no great necessity of doubling of files.	The difference between this and the former motion, is the difference of hands. And by this means, those files that stood before, now move; and they which moved, now stand, as appeareth by the figure. They are reduced by commanding *Files as you were,* or *Ranks to the right double.*

8	7	6	5	4	3	2	1			1	2	3	4	5	6	7	8
.	A	.	A	.	A	.	A			A	.	A	.	A	.	A	.
	A		A		A		A			A		A		A		A	
.	a	.	a	.	a	.	a			a	.	a	.	a	.	a	.
	a		a		a		a			a		a		a		a	
.	a	.	a	.	a	.	a			a	.	a	.	a	.	a	.
	a		a		a		a			a		a		a		a	
.	a	.	a	.	a	.	a			a	.	a	.	a	.	a	.
	a		a		a		a			a		a		a		a	
.	a	.	a	.	a	.	a			a	.	a	.	a	.	a	.
	a		a		a		a			a		a		a		a	
.	a	.	a	.	a	.	a			a	.	a	.	a	.	a	.
	a		a		a		a			a		a		a		a	
.	a	.	a	.	a	.	a			a	.	a	.	a	.	a	.
	a		a		a		a			a		a		a		a	
.	a	.	a	.	a	.	a			a	.	a	.	a	.	a	.
	a		a		a		a			a		a		a		a	

They are reduced by commanding *Files to the left as you were.*	*Half*

Half files, to the right hand double the front.

Thus the middle-men double the first rank on the right hand. The other three ranks double the three following ranks, as is manifest in the figure. To reduce them, the word is

Half files as you were.

Unlesse it be better (and so I conceive it) to cause them that double, to stand : and the first division to advance.

Half files, to the left hand double the front.

This motion onely differeth from the former in the hand. There be also doublings of ranks by the half files entire to the right, or left, or both by division : But because the files (especially of Cuirassiers) are seldome above five deep, the doubling of ranks, half files, &c. is little used.

The reducing of them hath been shewed in the former motion.

Bringers up, to the right hand double the front.

In this motion, the last rank passeth into the first, and so successively, as the figure sheweth it.

It is of good use: yet because it is very troublesome for the horse to perform, (especially in reducing them) it may be used, or omitted, as shall be thought fit. They are reduced by saying, *Bringers up, as you were.*

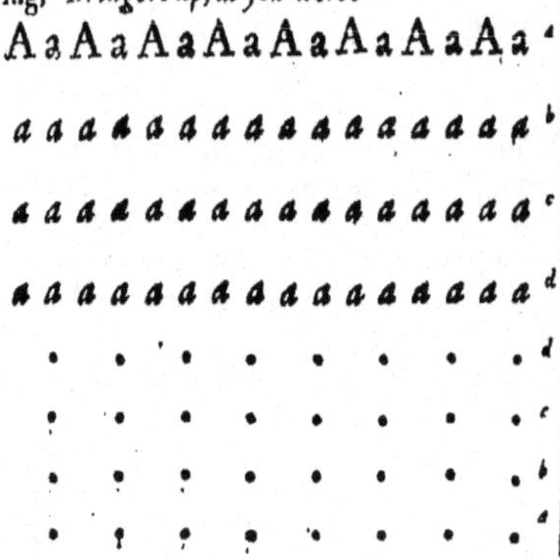

Files, to the left hand countermarch.

Though it were fit to begin with the right hand, yet for the convenient turning of the horse to the left, I think it not amisse to preferre the left

The figure representeth the *Chorean* manner.

There be also countermarches after the *Macedonian* and *Lacedemonian* wayes, and those in ranks as well as files, which are here omitted for brevity sake.

Files, close to the right and left to your close order.

Being about to wheel the company, they must be closed, first the files, and then the ranks. And being to open them again, the ranks are first to be opened, and then the files.

All the files close from the right and left, towards the middle of the body.

Ranks, close forwards, to your close order.

All the ranks move forwards, saving the first which standeth. The second rank having their distance, stand; so all the rest. Now the horse being to wheel, it must be considered that it cannot be performed by them in such exact manner, and so strait a room as the foot : therefore the Commander is to ride a reasonable compasse, that so they may do it with convenience.

To the left hand wheel.

Becaufe *Melzo* and *Bafta* would have the horfe in all their wheelings to do it by the left (which indeed is the readier way unleffe the ground or other hindrance will not permit it) I have omitted the wheeling to the right, which in order fhould go firft.

All the body moveth to the left, upon the left file-leader, as the centre. Then to wheel as they were.

There is also wheeling to the right, or left a-bout, wheeling wings into the front, &c. which are here omitted for brevitie.

To reduce them, firft the ranks are to be open-ed, (as abovefaid) then the files, which bringeth them to their firft form.

In opening the ranks, the beft (if not the one-ly) way is to do it by opening forward.

These and the like motions are directed and commanded by the voice of the Commander: but becaufe the voice fometime cannot be heard (efpecially in groffe bodies) by reafon of the clafhing of armour, trampling or neying of horfes, or tumultuous found, or noife of the multitude, (and that efpecially in fight) b Antiquitie hath invented helps; making three kinds of militarie fignes or directions :

1. *Vocall*, which is by the commanders voice, prohounced by the inferiour officers to the eare.
2. *Semivocall*, by trumpet or other warlike inftrument, to the eare likewife.
3. *Mute*, by fignes to the eye; as the enfigne, &c.

The Cavallrie therefore muft be taught c diftinctly to know the feverall founds of the trumpet; as when to clap on their faddle, when to mount, when to repair to the Cornet, when to troop away, when to give a charge, when to retreat, when to attend the watch, and the like. All which being the lowder voice of the Commander, d they muft punctually obferve and obey.

Now, howfoever I have here propounded a companie of 64. horfe; to be exercifed in the motions, and thofe of 8. in file (as I fee it obferved by e fome) yet the generall opinion is, that they ought not to be deeper then 5. in file, though the companie confift of 100. horfe.

Every fuch companie muft be furnifhed with

A Captain.	*Two Trumpeters.*
A Lieutenant.	*A Clerk.*
A Cornet.	*A Saddler.*
A Quartermafter,	*A Chirurgeon.*
Three Corporalls,	*A Farrier.*

When the companie be f to march, they are to be divided into 3 equall parts (and each of thefe is called a fquadron) according to the number of the Corporalls; and thefe are diftinguifhed by the names of the Captains, Lieutenants, and Cornets fquadron. The firft fquadron to be led by the Captain, the fecond by the Cornet, the third by the eldeft Corporall. The Lieutenant and Quartermafter are to come in the rear. And when they come to be exercifed (or to do fervice) the Captains fquadron ftands, and the other fquadrons fleeve up on the left hand, and fo they become a *Battalia*. As for their marching in groffe, that comes to be fpoken of in the next part.

things) he is fingular, and diffenteth from others.   f About the manner of marching of a companie of horfe, there is much difagreement among authori. *Melzo, Bafta,* and *Walhaufen* would have them to march in one entire deduction (not by fquadrons) the Captain to march firft, next after him two attendants with fpare horfes, they beating his armour: then the Trumpeters, then the Cornet, in the firft rank of horfe. But *Walhaufen* placeth the Lieutenant next after the Trumpeters, before the Cornet: all others place him (as he ought to be) in the rear. *Flaminio de la Croce* would have them march in foure divifions, and every Corporall to lead one; but this (the Corporalls being leaders of files) diffordereth their ranks. I follow that order which is prefcribed to be generally obferved by the councell of warre.

Side notes:

a *Vox autem percipi interdum non poteft, aut propter armorum fonitum, aut propter equorum tranfitum, & hinnitum, & multitudinis ftrepitum, &c.* Ælian. cap. 35

b *Nam cum voce fola inter prælium non tumultu regi multitudo non poffit, &c. antiquus omnium gentium ufus invenit, &c.*

Tria genera fignorum, Vocalis, femivocalis, muta, &c. Veget. lib.3 c 5.

c *Præcipies autem ut perfecte cognofcant buccinæ fonum, ut ubi confiftere eos jubet, confiftant, &c.* Leo Tact. cap. 9, 82.

d *Intenti ad ducis non fignum modo, fed nutum.* Curtius 3.

e *Walhaufen would have the Harquebufiers to be 8. in file, and the Cuiraffiers 10. lib. 2. cap. 2, & 3. But therein, (as in divers other*

The

The second Part.

Of Marching.

THE ARGUMENT.

 Aving shewed in the first part, how the Cavallrie is to be levied, it followeth now to speak of their manner of marching : a matter of no small [a] consequence; in the well ordering whereof, oftentimes (especially upon occasion of sudden charges) the safetie of the troops, or of the whole armie consisteth. For the orderly handling whereof I purpose to direct my discourse to these 3 heads.

     1 the knowledge, of the wayes, and discoverie of the enemies designes, and residence.

2. The conducting of the troops to their Rendez-vous, and their orders.

3. The particular distribution of the whole train upon the way; And the scouts or fore-runners. And how they are to march in an open or strait countrey, by day or night.

CHAP. I.
Of Guides.

For the knowledge of the wayes (a [a] matter of great importance, either to prevent the taking of one way for another in marching, or in pursuing the enemie, he having received the charge and flying by unusuall wayes) the use of maps may somewhat help, but (being too generall) is not sufficient. And therefore the Waggon-master is to provide good guides, of the inhabitants of those places where the march is to be, which may be able to give certain and particular information concerning the [b] high-wayes and crosse-wayes, how many there be of them; whether they be even, large, and free: or straight, hillie, or impeached with difficult passages. Also concerning ditches and rivers, whether there be bridges or not. And if there be divers wayes, which is the most safe and shortest, or most exposed to the enemies advenues or approches, or most commodious for the baggage. Whether there be requisite commoditie for the lodgings, as forrage, water, &c, Insomuch as they may be able to know every hedge or ditch, and all other particulars. And that you may be assured of their fidelitie, and the truth of their informations, it is good to have them to be souldiers in pay; or where they are not, to take them of the [c] boores or inhabitants (as aforesaid) from place to place, keeping them separated from each other. And if they differ, either from the souldiers which serve for guides, or from each other, they must be confronted; and by the mutuall consent of all, the best way is to be resolved on. These guides usually (to prevent their running away, which they will often do if they see an opportunitie of escaping) are led bound, [d] or at least committed to the custodie of some souldier. Recompence is promised them if they do their endeavour, and punishment threatned if they direct amisse.

CHAP. II.
Of Intelligence.

Every good commander must have these two grounds for his actions; 1. the knowledge of his own forces, and wants, (knowing that the enemie may have notice thereof, and therefore must he be alwayes studying for remedies, if the enemie should come suddenly upon him) 2. The assurance of the condition and estate of the enemie, his commodities, and necessities, his counsels and designes; thereby begetting divers occasions, which afterward bring forth victories. [a] And becaus the commoditie of spies cannot alwayes be had ; some of the enemies men must be assayed to be taken, from whom there may be drawn a relation of the estate of the adverse part, and this exploit is called [b] taking of intelligence, a dutie of great importance, (whereon the deliberations which are to be taken do depend) and also of much travell and danger.

     To effect this, an expert officer, with 20 or 25 of the [c] best mounted, stoutest, and hardiest Harquebusiers (or mixt of Cuirassiers and Harquebusiers, according to *Melzo*) with two Trumpets are to be employed. These are to carrie with them some refreshment for themselves and their horses; to that purpose retiring themselves into some wood, or shadie place; placing good Centinells upon trees. If they find the enemie marching, they shall follow him on either flank (as opportunitie shall direct them) or on the reat, or meet him on the front, assaying to take some that are disbanded, or some forrager. In the night they must approch the enemies armie, assaying to take some Sentinell, or some disbanded souldier in some of the houses thereabout. And because it well may fall out that (after the taking of some prisoner) the troop shall be charged by the enemie; the Chief (which must be valiant, [d] and abundant in resolutions and inventions of stratagems to make his retreat by some woodie place) shall send (or first there leave them) foure of his best, and best mounted souldiers with a Trumpet; with order, that when they see the troop coming, charged by the enemie, they shew themselves, the trumpet sounding. For, it being an usuall thing in militarie courses to go and observe who they be which appear, the enemie by this means makes *Alto,* (or a stand) for fear of some *embuscado* which gives leisure to the troop to advance their retreat: and the said foure souldiers may make their retreat, either severally, or together, safe enough, by reason of their good horses. If the enemie be likely to come from divers parts, the like number would be sent to each suspected place. These should be sent before with the Quartermasters which go to make the quarters, that so they might have two or three houres refreshment, before they go to take intelligence. If the armie be lodged in a very suspicious place; after the first troop so sent out, a second shall be sent; but neither of them knowing of each others sending out. If the armie be to march the next day, the chiefs of the said troops must know towards what place the march is intended.

CHAP. III.

Of the order of Marching.

THe Commissarie Generall, grounding himself upon good informations, is to give the orders in writing for the manner of marching, as well of the souldiers as the baggage. Every Captain is to receive his written directions overnight, that so, the signe given, he may appear at the Rendez-vous in such rank and place as shall be commanded him.

[a] Every armie is divided into three parts; The vanguard, battel, and rear. That part of the armie which is most exposed to the enemie (and that most usually is the front) should be the best; and therefore all chiefs desire the vanguard. The manner therefore is (for generall satisfaction) that they which this day had the van, to morrow have the rear; and they which had the rear, the battel. So changing alternatively; except the Lord Generalls guard (consisting of two troops, as *Melzo* hath it) or the Generalls regiment (according to C. *Bingham*) which hath alwayes the vanguard. And if the enemie should change place, and from your front become to be upon your rear, whereby the rear (as most dangerous) becomes most honourable; that Captain which to day hath led the battaillon, to morrow (in stead of the vanguard) may challenge the rear.

The scouts alter their course also, and attend the enemies proceedings on the rear.

If occasion be (in time of march) to send out one or more troops for some service, they are to observe the same orders. But the armie being come to their quarter, and occasion being to send out [b] all or part of the Cavallrie upon some exploit; that troop which first appeareth at the place of Rendez-vous shall be appointed by the Commissarie Generall (who is to be there) to the first place; the second to the second place. If two troops come together, at the same instant, they shall cast lots.

By this means, every man desiring honour, they will be the readier to appear in due time. The same course shall be taken when the troops are to be sent upon some embuscado, convoy, or the like. If the march be but of one day, he which commandeth shall appoint the best experienced and ablest to lead; [c] who is to be in the rear, returning back to the quarter. And these may have private order to be at the place of Rendezvous sooner then the rest, to avoid jealousies.

The vanguard, battaillon, and rear, must be divided from each other 300 paces.

CHAP. IIII.

Of Scouts or Discoverers.

TO be secured from unexpected assaults of the enemie, neither the armie nor the Cavallrie alone, no not a companie, must march without [a] discoverers: which must be sent out, not onely by the direct way where the enemie is like to come, or you are to march, but to scoute all the by-wayes on either side. And sometime the first discoverers are seconded by a second companie, to secure the march.

They that shall be employed in this service must be choice men, valiant, vigilant and discreet: such as neither fear nor misconceit can easily distract. They must see that with their own eyes which they inform, the least errour of theirs misleading the whole bodie. Those select men appointed for this service, are to be [b] led by an able officer; it being a task so difficult, that many

haue

have loft that reputation by it which they had been long in gaining of. This officer ſhall ſend word of what he diſcovereth; and what he ſeeth not himſelf, he is to ſignifie it as ſo reported to him; and having ſeen it, then to certifie it as for certain.

CHAP. V.
Of the order of marching by day.

THe march muſt be ſo ordered as the companies may readily (from that order) be brought into a good form of battel, upon occaſion of a ſudden charge. The Cavallrie (ſuppoſed to conſiſt of 40 troops, and the countrey ſpacious) is to be divided into two bodies of 20 troops a-piece. *Melzo* would have 3 troops of Harquebuſiers in front of the vanguard, which *Baſta* and *Walhauſen* are againſt, becauſe they are (for the moſt part) but ill armed. Theſe two diviſions are to march in even front, 150 paces divided. Coming to ſtrait paſſages, the right wing is to march before the left. The officers muſt ſuffer none of the baggage nor any other to intermingle with their troops.

The Captain of Harquebuſiers which hath the vanguard (or one of them in that diviſion, when the Cuiraſſiers have it) b muſt ſend out a Corporall with 15 horſe and a good guide, ſome league before; whereof two ſhall be ſent out directly before him; two towards the right, and other two towards the left; c to diſcover among the woods and valleys, and to get intelligence at any dwelling houſes or villages, adviſing the Corporall of what they diſcover. Who is from time to time to adviſe the chief, which is to march at the head of the firſt troop.

After theſe 15 he is to ſend out 4 others, led by a ſufficient ſouldier, to bring reports of what thoſe 15 ſhall diſcover; the rather becauſe the enemie might come upon them upon the flanks, after the firſt 15 were paſt.

The Captain of the Harquebuſiers which hath the rear of the left wing, muſt leave a Corporall with 15 horſe a mile behind him. Of theſe 15, two are to be ſome 12 or 14 ſcore behind the reſt, to give notice if the enemie follow them in the rear.

d The Captain which leads in front muſt march ſo as the other troops muſt keep foot with him; and paſſing over a bridge or narrow paſſage, muſt make *Alto* ſo ſoon as he is over, or in the plain, leaving a ſouldier at the bridge or ſtrait, which ſhall give him knowledge ſo ſoon as the rear be paſt over or through. e And if in theſe ſtrait paſſages there be any advenues by which the enemie might charge you, thoſe muſt be prepoſſeſſed by Harquebuſiers, or Dragons, alighting, and keeping themſelves upon ſome height, or in ſome valley, or behind ſome hedge or ditch, to ſecure their flanks.

Every troop is to leave 100 paces diſtance between each other, and are to ſuffer no baggage nor others to trouble them, as aboveſaid.

CHAP. VI.
The order of marching by night.

UPon occaſion of marching with all or part of the Cavallrie by night, the companies are punctually appointed their places of march by written orders delivered to their officers. Before the troops, a Corporall with 12 or 15 Harquebuſiers is to be ſent, by the ſpace of half a league, to diſcover and take intelligence at the houſes, whether there be any news of the enemie. And paſſing by places which are at the enemies devotion, ſome of them muſt have the language, and feigne themſelves friends, the better to know what paſſeth.

Not long after theſe, foure others are to follow, as in the former chapter. Beſides, a choſen troop of Cuiraſſiers are to be ready, led by a Captain of ſpeciall deſert, with order to a charge reſolutely upon any adverſarie; and theſe are to march 150 paces before the reſt.

The chief Commander is to march at the head of the firſt troop which followeth the ſaid choſen troop of 60 Cuiraſſiers, and with him one of the beſt ſouldiers of every troop, to carrie the orders (upon all occaſions) to their Captains: ſending before him foure of his ableſt men, to give him notice if the ſaid ſelect troop of 60 Cuiraſſiers charge the enemie: which if it happen, he ſhall caſt his companie out of the way, and charge the enemie on the flank; and ſo the reſt of the troops, obſerving that they intermix not their troops.

The troops muſt not leave ſuch diſtances between each other as in the day march, unleſſe they heare news of the enemies approch. b They muſt march with all poſſible ſilence. At any by-way, the firſt company muſt leave a ſouldier at the entrance thereof, which ſhall be relieved or changed by the next company, and ſo ſucceſſively untill all be paſt. Coming into open and champion places, the officers ſhall draw up their troops, and cauſe them to march in ſquare bodies, well cloſed, having regard that none ſleep. The ſpare horſes or pages muſt not march at the heads of the troops. If the enemie charge the rear, the chief officer in the rear ſhall cauſe the laſt company to face about; and ſo the reſt, if need be: but thoſe companies which were in front muſt not come to the rear, for avoiding of diforder, and left the enemy cunningly make an alarm in the rear, when he meaneth to charge the front. In the rear of all, a Corporall with 15 horfe fhall march as above-mentioned, with a guide. The day being come, tho faid 60 Cuiraffiers fhall return to their feverall companies. If the companies refrefh themfelves in the night, they muft not be fuffered to unfaddle their horfes, nor difarm themfelves. The guides (diverfe of them) muft go before the troops, whether on foot or on horfe-back, guarded by two fouldiers which know the language, and no other to fpeak to them. c Thefe are diligently to obferve them whether they feem doubtfull, looking here and there, as doubting of the way, and thereof fhall prefently certifie the officer, that he may call others, to be affured.

c Interdum autem importa ni-stieius plus promittit, & credit se seire qua nescit. Veg l.3,c.6.

CHAP. VII.
How the baggage is to march.

AS little baggage as poffible may be muft be conducted with the Cavallrie. It is the Waggon-mafters charge to order it for the march. Firft, the Generalls baggage is to march, then the Lieutenant Generalls, then the Commiffary Generalls, and fo the other officers in their degrees.

The place of march is uncertain; a but alwayes it muft be moft remote from danger. If the danger be in the front, it marcheth in the rear, &c. The Waggon-mafter (or with fome the Provoft) muft fee that all march in their appointed place, and disband not. A company of Harque-bufiers is to guard the baggage. The horfe-boyes march after the waggons, and muft not be fuffered to march among the troops.

a Auuertends ancora, che tutti li impe-dimenti & ar-tiglierie sempre camino da quel-le parte, che non sia volta verso al nemico Cataneo, c. 8. This agreeth with Ælian directions, c.51. Impedimenta,&c.

The third Part.

Of Encamping.

THE ARGUMENT.

THe next part to be handled (according to our former diftribution) is Encamping. In the skilfull performance whereof, the military prudence and good judgement of the Commander of an army chiefly appeareth. And herein three things are principally confiderable.

1. In what place, and by whom the quarter is to be made, and how diftributed.
2. The manner of fecuring the quarter, by guards, fentinels, difcoverers, fpies, &c.
3. Of diflodging, and the way how to perform it.

CHAP. I.
Of making the quarters.

IN a the choife of a fitting place for encamping or quartering, regard muft be had, Firft, to the commoditie of the fouldiers; Secondly, to the fituation; to be able to refift the enemie: For experience teacheth what benefit or loffe an army may receive by a good or bad quartering, and hereof hiftories yield a world of examples.

a Castra tuto tem-pore facienda funt loco: ubi & ligno-rum & pabuli & aqua suppetas co-pia. Et si dinuius commorandum eft, loci falubritai eligetur, &c. Veg.lib.1.cap.22

To lodge or encamp the Cavallrie, a fpeciall care muft be had of the commodity of water, and where they may be under fhelter: for one cold or rainy night might ruine the Cavallrie, nothing hurting a horfe fooner then cold or wet. By this means the fouldier fhall find forrage at hand, and needeth not to go feek it abroad with his horfe of fervice, all not having nags. When the horfe be lodged in feverall quarters, two fouldiers of every quarter attend the perfon of the Generall, or the chief Commander, to carry any fudden orders to their feverall quarters. But of fuch companies as are quartered near him, b one is fufficient. When all the Cavallry is lodged together, the Lieutenant Generall, Commiffary Generall, and Quartermafter Generall are ufually lodged near the Generall, for the better diftributing of the Generalls orders.

b Unus ex omni-bus manipulu im-peraios in diem excubat. Polyb.

The appointing of the quarters belongeth to the Commiffary Generall and the Marfhall, by whofe directions the Quartermafter Generall proceedeth. It is fit for them to have fome demon-ftration on paper, of the place beforehand; and to know the commodities and difcommodities, alfo advenues of the enemy; wherein the guides can better direct them then the ufuall maps, which (if not falfe) are too generall. When the Quartermafter Generall c goeth before to make the quarters, not onely the particular Quartermafters, but alfo two fouldiers of every company are to go with him; which then go back again to conduct their refpective companies to their affigned quarters;

c Cum verò ap-propinquaverint ubi castra ponen-da, præunt Tri-bunæ, & Centu-rionum illi, qui ad hoc munus semper electi sunt; &c. Polyb.

especially in the night. The Provost (or rather the Waggon-master) sendeth one of his men to take notice of the place for the lodging of the baggage, who afterward conducteth him thither; where he then assigneth the Sutlers (or victuallers) their quarter, and causeth all carts or waggons to be removed out of the streets, lest an alarm be given.

CHAP. II.

Of distributing the quarters.

GReat discretion must be used in appointing to every one such quarter as is fitting and conformable to the quality of his person, and convenience of the place. The best way to avoid suspicion of partialitie is, that such as be ill lodged now, be better accommodated the next time. The market-place (for the conveniency of all, and for safetie) is to be in the middle; but so as no streets run through it leading to the Rendezvous or place of arms.

When the quarter is to be in some suspected place, it should (if possibly it could) be made in the day time, before the approach of the night, that so the fittest place for the alarm place might be made choise of, and also for the corps-du-guard; also the better to discover and observe the approches of the enemy, and to appoint the stands of the Sentinells; that so the souldiers finding all things ready, be not put to find out their lodgings in the dark with lighted straw, in danger to fire the houses: besides, a Lieutenant with 25 Harquebusiers useth to be sent out before, and to place themselves beyond the further side of the village where the quarter shall be, placing Sentinells a good distance before them, to prevent the enemies sudden approch on that part. The best house must be appointed for the Generall, as near the Corps-du-guard as may be; the rest of the officers are to be accommodated in their order. Every Captain must lodge among his souldiers. The troops, being come neat to the quarter, make *Alto*; and receiving information by the Quarter-master Generall, or one of the particular Quartermasters, that the quarters are ready, the Chief giveth license to the Captains to enter their quarters. They which have the guard are to be conducted to the place by the Quartermaster Generall. But if the army be encamped in the field, the Cavallrie is to be quartered, according to the [b] manner of quartering of a regiment, [c] represented in *figure* 4, part 3. chap. 2. And of the whole army in Figure 5.

in figure by *Lipsius* in his book *De milit. Rom. lib.5 dial.4.* Also by Sir *H. Savile*, in his annotations upon *Tacitus*. And by Sir *Cl. Edmonds* in his observations upon *Cæsars Commentaries, lib.2.cap 9.* And described by *Veget. lib 3.cap.8.* c For the modern quarterings, see *S. Stevin* his castrametation. Also *D. de Soktnine*, and others.

CHAP. III.

Of the necessitie of securing the quarters.

NOthing sooner deceiveth an unexperienced Captain, then to perswade himself that he is superiour in forces, and in advantage of place, and so farre distant from his enemie as he cannot, or dare not assail him. Upon which supposition the [a] surprisings of quarters are often grounded, it being no marvell that secure and disordered men should be assaulted by well ordered men and resolute; among the Cavallrie especially, where the souldier cannot arm himself without help: his horse-boy nor himself being scarce themselves, (as but newly rouzed out of their sleep by the alarm) can hardly tell where to find bridle or saddle, or light; so as the enemy is upon their jacks before they can mount, or at least unite themselves together.

These things oftentimes happen, but are justly derided by good souldiers, [b] and therefore all diligence must be used at all times as if the enemy were at hand, ready to set upon the quarters every moment.

CHAP. IIII.

Of the manner of securing the quarters.

ALl the diligences used about securing of the quarters, seem onely to serve for the gaining of time, [a] and that the enemy may not charge you on the sudden, so as the souldiers have not convenient time to arm themselves, mount their horses, and assemble at the place of arms. To effect this, there is no better way then to [b] make sure the enemies approches. If the quarter be in a suspected place, the companies of Harquebusiers are to be quartered in the adventes of the village, the Lances (if any be) and Cuirassiers in the middle.

At the entrances of all the streets, either trees or [c] waggons are to be placed acrosse, giving order to the Harquebusiers to guard those passages, and that none of them mount on horseback without speciall order: that so, the rest may have time to assemble at the place of arms, if the enemy come

ready for battell, to guard them which (behind them) wrought about the trenches. And this was done by every century by turns; every souldier becoming a pioner for the time. Ibid. cap. 25. c For a sudden defence of the quarter (it being in a champain countrey, destitute of any other) it hath been usuall to enclose the quarter with waggons and carts. So did the Helvetians (now called Swissers) as *Cæsar* recordeth it, *Commint. cap.1a.* And to this purpose, *vide Veget. lib.3.cap.1a.* Perse (imitantes Romanos) ductu fossis castra constituunt; & quia armosa sunt propè omnia, saccos quos habent portavērunt, eos pulvulenta (qua effoditur) terra complent, aorumque cumulis aggerem faciunt. Ibid.

THis Regiment confifteth of foure troops of horfe, *viz.* two of *Cuiraffiers*, and two of *Harquebufiers*: which Regiment containeth in breadth (or front) from A. to B. 700. foot, and in depth (or length) from B. to C. 300. foot: from A. to D. is 205 foot in breadth for one company of *Cuirafiers*, which confifteth of 80 horfe, together with 80 nags, which have five files of huts, and five files of horfe, which *Curafsiers* are quartered (or lodged) on the right hand of the Regiment.

From E to Z is 115 foot in breadth for a company of *Harquebufiers*, which confifteth of 100 horfe, and it hath three files of huts and horfes.

From A to G is the fpace of ground where the Collonell of the Regiment is lodged, on the right hand of thefe foure companies, and the faid enclofure for the Collonel is 70 foot broad, from A to G.

From G to H is 40 foot in depth (or length) for the faid enclofure for the Collonell; and fo are all the other enclofures of the Officers.

From H to I is 20 foot in breadth, for the ftreet between the Collonells Enclofure, and the Enclofure for the Lieutenant and Cornet of the faid Collonells company (which are both lodged in one Enclofure, marked I K) which hath alfo 70 foot in breadth, as that of the Collonel; which Enclofure is divided into two parts: The Lieutenant being lodged on the right hand, and hath 40 foot in breadth for his Enclofure: And the Cornet on the left hand (with one of the Trumpeters) having the other 30 foot in breadth of the faid Enclofure; which maketh 70 foot for them both.

From K to L is another ftreet of twenty foot broad, to the enclofure marked L M. L M is the enclofure where the Quartermafter is lodged, with two other horfemen which he pleafeth to admit of, which is 25 foot broad, and 40 foot long, as the reft. Their hut (within the faid Enclofure) being 12 foot fquare for them three, and their ftable is 25 foot broad for their fix horfes.

From M to N is 30 foot for the ftreet between the Quartermafters enclofure, and the firft hutts for the horfemen, marked N.

From N to O is 180 foot for the quartering of the files of huts for the horfmen, *viz.* for 16 huts, and their 32 horfes in a file, agreeable to the Regiments of Infantery: That fo, where the Regiments of Cavallry are to be lodged in the champaine ground among the Infanterie, they might all make one and the fame line before and behind the Regiments. And through the faid two Troops of *Cuirafsiers* there be two ftreets marked P. which ftreets are of 13 foot broad and the huts of the horfemen are ten fort broad, and 8 foot long for one horfeman and his boy. And between two huts there is two foot of fpace for the drain of rain water, dropping from the thatch or covers of the huts. Thefe huts have their chief doores or paffages towards the heads of their horfes, and a fmall one opening into the ftreet, where they lay their hay and ftraw every one behind his own hut.

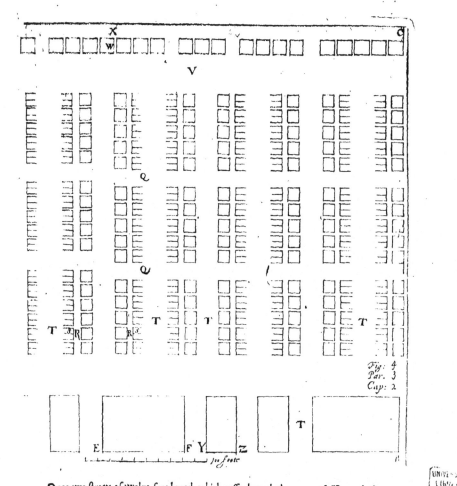

Fig: 4
Par: 3
Cap: 2

Q are two ſtreets of twelve foot broad, which paſſe through the troops of *Harquebuſiers*.

R is a ſtreet of five foot broad, between the horſmens huts, and the mangers for their horſes.

S is ten foot for the Stables for their horſes, which horſes are placed with their heads toward their huts, and every horſe hath 4 foot in breadth for his litter, and 8 foot for the two horſes; according to the length of their huts. And more ground then eight foot they muſt not take; for otherwiſe it would cauſe a great diſorder and confuſion, not obſerving the ſaid preciſe meaſures.

T is a ſtreet of 20 foot broad between the heels of their horſes: in which ſtreet they mount and alight off their horſes; which ſtreet they are bound to keep clean, and to carry away the dung every two or three dayes.

V is 30 foot in breadth for the ſtreet called the Victuallers (or Sutlers) ſtreet.

W are the Sutlers huts being ten foot ſquare, and more room they muſt not take, unleſſe (when they have many Penſioners) the Quartermaſter give them a foot or two more in breadth, but not in depth, to obſerve the meaſure of 300 foot in the depth of the Regiment, as the Infantery.

X is ten foot of ground behind the Sutlers huts, for a place for the Sutlers, the horſmen and their wives to dreſſe their victuals. And in no other place of the Quarter muſt any fire be made. Neither are they to caſt any filth,&c. within the Quarter, but to carry it to the place appointed thereunto, upon pain of a fine, which the Provoſt taketh.

E F is the encloſure of the Captain of a troop of *Harquebuſiers*, being of the ſame breadth and depth as thoſe of the Capt. of *Cuiraſſiers*, viz. 70. foot broad, and 40 foot deep. And the ancienteſt Captain of *Harquebuſiers*, or *Cuiraſſiers* cloſeth the battailon of the Regiment on the left hand, at the corner marked B.

F Y is a ſtreet of twenty foot broad, to the Lieutenant of the troop of *Harquebuſiers* his encloſure Y.

Y Z is 25 foot in breadth for the encloſure of the ſaid Lieutenant, where alſo are placed his foure horſes; having in depth 40 foot. And the Cornets of the troops of *Harquebuſiers* are lodged on the right hand in the two firſt huts of the horſmen, and that to place his three horſes, and the fourth horſe is the Trumpeters, who alwayes lodgeth with the Cornet. Theſe companies of *Harquebuſiers* have alſo 180 foot depth for the quartering of their three files of huts marked (in the *Cuiraſſiers*) N O. but theſe have but 15 huts in every file for 30 horſe: having alſo two ſtreets (as the *Cuiraſſiers*) through them marked Q. being 12 foot broad (as aboveſaid) leaving three foot of ſpace between their huts for the drain (whereas the Cuiraſſiers have but two foot) their huts are alſo of ten foot broad and 8 foot deep for two *Harquebuſiers*, and 8 foot for the litter of their two horſes, and ten foot for their ſtable. And five foot for a ſtreet between their huts, and the mangers of their horſes: their Sutlers ſtreets, and Sutlers huts, &c. are as the *Cuiraſſiers*.

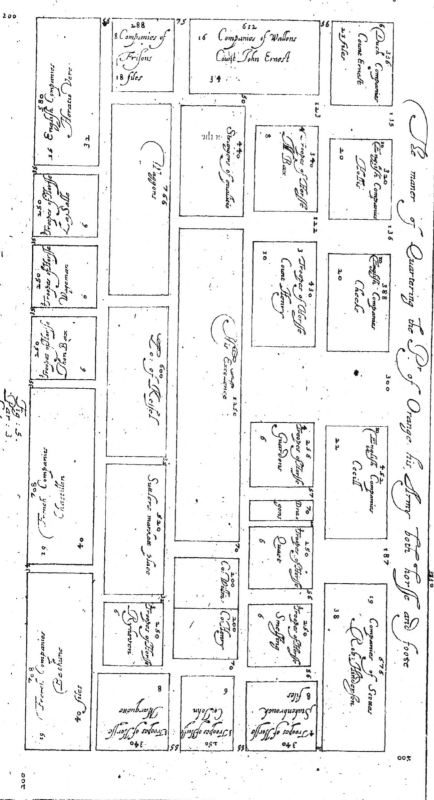

upon them; unto which a new passage must be cut, for the more privacie and security. If there be Dragons, then they are to guard the said approches: If Infantery, then it is their task to do it.

If the situation of the place be such as that the enemy may environ it round, the usuall entrances or approches to the village are to be stopped up, and new ones cut in some secret places, as gardens or the like, distant from the usuall wayes, that so the enemy may be afraid to charge home a Centinell or Corps-du-guard, thereby to enter with them as they retreat. The quarters are to be well barricadoed about, except the new cut passages leading to the Rendezvous.

CHAP. V.
Of the Rendez-vous or alarm place.

THe alarm place is that place without the village, where the souldiers are to assemble to withstand an assailing enemy, being a place of great consequence.

In the election of this place, consideration must be had of the situation of the villages and countrey, whether it be large or strait; also of the time, whether it be by day or night: again, whether the Cavallrie be lodged together, or in severall villages. If together in one village, and in the night, (when the enemy may come upon them the more at unaware, as not being discoverable very farre) then this place must not be in the front of the village, as being too near the enemies approch, whereby it might be seised on by him, and so your men cut off one after another as they come thither to assemble themselves: but it must be on the sides or flanks of the village, though the baggage be hazarded; which [a] inviting the enemy to pillaging, often giveth him occasion of disorder. But in the day time it were best to be in front, shewing the more courage.

a This all ages have verified. The States men (by a stratagem) had surprised S. Hertogen-Bosh, anno 1585. but by reason of the covetousnesse of the souldiers (neglecting their charges to fall to pillaging) were beaten out again with losse. Metteren lib. 12.

If the Cavallrie be quartered in diverse villages (which often happeneth, especially in places little suspected) the quality of the countrey must be considered. Some villages may be backed with rivers, and so give but one entrance to the enemie: then the generall place of arms or rendez-vous shall be in the center. And those villages which are exposed to the first brunt, shall be as Corpsdu-guards to assure the rest. These (upon alarm given) must assemble in their particular alarm places, from thence they shall advance, united to receive the charge, though the enemy farre exceed them in number: and must sustain him so long, till they may be assured that the rest are all met at the generall Rendez-vous, whether (being forced by the enemy) they shall retreat by little and little, the other advancing to relieve them, If the countrey be open, so as the enemy may assail which he please, then they must use those diligences as when the Cavallrie is lodged altogether in one village. They which are first assaulted must make resistance, untill the other be met at the generall Rendez-vous.

Touching the order of their assembling together in the alarm place, the Commissary Generall, or Quartermaster Generall, overnight appointeth a certain place for every troop, where they shall stand, which way faced, &c.

CHAP. VI.
Of the Guards.

THe Commissary Generall is to keep account of the [a] Guards, and to give orders requisite to those that are to have the guard: wherein he may employ one or more companies, according to occasions. The Corps-du-guard must be in the middle of the village. The guards, being disposed in their places, must be every night visited by the Commissary Generall (which often the Lieutenant Generall, and sometime the Generall himself ought to do) to keep the souldiers in the greater aw. The Generalls company is exempt from the ordinary guards and convoyes, because they must be a guard to the Generall, (unlesse the Generall go in person) and so is the Lieutenant Generalls company.

a Of the guards, and means of securing the quarters, used among the Romanes, Vegetius handleth at large, lib. 3. cap. 8.

The companies entring the guard, must be compleatly armed, and sound their trumpets; their Lieutenant taking information of all things from the Lieutenant which goeth from the guard, and then certifying his Captain; who is to acquaint his superiour officers with all occurrences, and with the reports of such as went to discover and scowre the high-wayes, also of the convoyes and other duties.

If the Cavallrie lodge in severall villages (which ever must not be farre distant from each other) in every village a company must have the guard and Sentinells.

b Edict for Martiall law, art. 58.

[b] The Captains, officers, and souldiers which have the guard must be armed all night, and have their horses at hand, ready bridled, observing all possible silence.

In the day time, if there be any open champain within half a league (or thereabout) of the quarter, the company which hath the guard shall send out a Corporall with twelve or fifteen horse, which shall hide himself in some covert place near the entrance of the said champain. There he shall place double Sentinells in some eminent place, who seeing some Cavallry, one shall go to descry them, the other shall go and tell the Corporall; who sending word to the Corps-du-guard, shall advance at large, sending out two horses to take knowledge of the said Cavallry. If there be

some.

some high tree near the place where the said Corporall stood, he may thereon place a Sentinell, and save the sending out of the said two Sentinels. These horse shall be changed (or relieved) twice a day, by those which have the guard. If the enemy charge them, they are to retreat to the said entrance, and there to entertain the enemy till they of the guard can be ready (upon the former notice given them) and come to second them.

If all the Cavallry go to oppose the enemy, the Captain of the guard shall have the vanguard. If more companies then one be employed for guard, that company shall have it, near which the alarm was given.

Sometime it so happeneth as that the troops come to their quarter in the night and in ill weather, so as the advenues cannot be observed, nor fitting places for the guards nor Sentinels : Then the Commissary Generall (or the Generall himself) is to go and appoint them as he shall judge most convenient : appointing to every company ten souldiers of guard, (more or lesse as need shall require) and commanding all to be in readinesse, giving order to the Corps-du-guard (as the onely remedy) that if the enemy assail the quarter, they go resolutely and charge him: which (besides the honour and reputation so gotten) oftentimes proveth [c] fortunate. Some use (to keep their souldiers awake) to sound the boute-selle at midnight, as if the enemy were at hand; but that might prove more dangerous then profitable : for after the first time , it maketh the souldiers secure and carelesse. Better it is that (after two or three houres refreshing) in such cases, the companies be caused to go out into the champain, every [d] souldier taking with him some oats and other refreshments; placing the Corps-du-guards as shall be thought fit, and not giving eare to the murmuring of the souldiers. But if the weather be rainy and tempestuous , such as that they must be under shelter, every officer (by certain houres) shall divide the night, and go from house to house, knocking and calling to the souldiers, causing them to saddle their horses. A while after him, another is to enter the houses, and see every souldier armed and ready to mount, punishing those that are sluggish.

c Audtes suru na jvvat.

d Si sint illa cutela, nihil nosturni aut diurni superventus hostium nocere possunt Veg.lib.3.cap.10

The Quartermasters shall also (by turns) visit the quarters and guards. The Chief himself is also to visit the souldiers, calling to one and to another with a loud voice, to make them the more attentive.

CHAP. VII.
Of the Sentinels.

SEeing [a] that they of the guard cannot be alwayes on horse-back, nor discover the enemy asarre off, to prevent a sudden surprise, Sentinels have been invented; which every Corps-du-guard setteth out of those souldiers which have the guard. These are usually placed [b] double, that while one goeth to certifie the Chief of the Corps-du-guard what he hath heard or seen, the other stayeth to observe new accidents which might happen.

a The Romanes manner of setting out of Sentinels, and all that belongeth to the watch, Vegetius sheweth, lib.3. cap.8.

They are placed where most high-wayes joyn, to possesse all the advenues, if they exceed not three hundred paces distance.

b Necessariis locis ac temporibus non modo simplices, verùm etiam duplices vigilia

Nearer to the Corps du-guard there useth to be placed a single Sentinell, to observe the motions of the other double.

Between these, another single Sentinell sometime is placed (when the double are somewhat further off to possesse some crosse way , or when for some other hinderance they are not in view of him) which may have both them and the nearest single Sentinell in view. So that every Sentinell must know that he is onely placed there to certifie the Corps-du-guard of all occurrences; so as (though he were provoked by any advantageous occasion) he must not stirre a foot; or else he committeth a [c] capitall crime. While the one is gone to relate his observation to the Corps-du-guard, if the second be forced by the enemie , he shall by little and little retreat to the said Corps-du-guard.

constituenda sunt, ut si qund alteram latus, ambos latera non possit. Leo Tact.cap. 14.31.

c That souldier which by day or night shall remove from the place where he was placed Sentinell by his Corporall, before he be by him called away or relieved, shall be punished with death, without favour. Edict.art.28. Pæna mortis apud Romanos, illi qui locum deseruisset aut omnino sugisset ex statione, Polyb. lib.r.

No Sentinell must alight from his horse, unlesse for naturall necessitie ; and then but one at once.

In the day time , the Sentinells are to be placed on high places to discover the further, but not on the high-wayes, lest they be surprised by forragers or others of the enemie, pretending to be friends : he shall therefore keep a stones cast out of the high-way, suffering none to accost him.

In the night (if it may be) they shall be placed in valleys, because from thence one seeth best what cometh from the higher ground. They shall suffer no person (whosoever he be) to enter or go out of the quarter; but causing him to stand at 30 or 40 paces distance from them, the one shall go and certifie his officer; who ([d] having the watch-word) shall go and take notice of him, and know his businesse in that place, and at that time.

d Since the Prince of Parma's time, the wresting the word, which were

The Sentinells are to be changed (or relieved) after this manner; The [e] houre being come, the

Sentinells have not been trusted with the word: by reason of a miscarriage at the siege at Tournay, which the States men relieved by wresting the word from a Sentinell.   e The Romanes divided their night (and so the day) into foure watches, every watch containing three artificiall houres, and unequall andplanetary. The first night watch ever begun at sunsetting; the second continued untill midnight : the rest accordingly. Every Sentinell watched three houres, and then was relieved. *In quatuor partes ad clepsydram sunt divisa vigilia, ut non ampliùs quàm tribus horis nocturnis, necesse sit vigilare. A tibicine omnes vigilia commutantur, & finitis horis à cornicine revocantur, Veg. lib.3.cap.8.*

Lieutenant parteth from the Corps-du-guard with that number of horse which are to stand Sentinell, the one half of these he committeth to a Corporall, or old expert souldier, which goeth with him (for the Cornet must not forsake his standard) the other moitie he retaineth to himself. This division made, the Lieutenant with his troop goeth one way, the Corporall with his, the other; encompassing the whole quarter, each of them having a trumpet with them. Thus they (riding one towards another) change the Sentinells from place to place, conducting the discharged Sentinells with them, till they meet each other.

The Captain having gone the first round, [f] the rounders are to be sent out, to see whether these Sentinels be vigilant. And sometimes foure other rounders are sent out, twice as farre beyond the Sentinells, as they are from the quarter, (twice at least in a night) to discover round about the quarter, and to observe whether the dogs bark more then usually, &c.

f The sending out of rounders was also used by the Romanes. *Idoneos tamen tribunos & probatissimos eligunt, qui vigilias circumeant, & renuntient si qua censerint culpa, quos circuitores appellabant.* Veg. ibid.

g *Equites extra villam nocturnas excubias facere debent.* Ibid.

If they observe any thing, one comes back to bring the news, the other three go on. In the day time, a Sentinell shall be placed on the top of the steeple of the village, where the quarter is, and a boore with him, as best knowing the passages and approaches. If the Sentinell which alwayes walks before the Corps-du-guard cannot heare him, another Sentinell shall be placed at the foot of the steeple, so that these three may understand each other, and (without losse of time) give notice to the Corps-du-guard. Besides, there ought to be double [g] Sentinells on horsback placed on high places without the quarter, to be able to discover the further.

The Generall hath alwayes a Sentinell at his tent, so hath the Lieutenant Generall, (taken out of their own guards) and so the Commissarie Generall. No Captain may have a Sentinell (not to overburden the souldiers) unlesse he command the quarter, or have the Cornet lodging with him : except the Captains of Harquebusiers which lodge in the advenues, that so they may the sooner have notice of an alarm.

The Commissarie Generall must shew the Captain that hath the guard, where the Sentinells for the quarter shall be placed. The one Sentinell (when they see men approching) shall withdraw himself somewhat from the other, towards the quarter; that so (if any violence be offered to the other) he may run to the Corps-du-guard.

They are not onely to certifie of the approch of the enemie or any other; but also are to observe the fires which they see, or the barking of dogs which they heare more then usuall, or shooting with canon or small shot afarre off, and of all to inform the Corps-du-guard.

If an alarm be given whilest the Lieutenant and Corporall aforesaid are about to change the Sentinels, they must presently send word to the quarter, and instantly hasten towards the place where the alarm is, leaving the Sentinells to stand somewhat the longer.

h *Castra muniri semper tutum est, &c. si enim aliquid adversum contingat, minus imperterriti est dicere aliquando, Non putaram.* Leo Tact. c. 10.

[h] To assure the quarter in an open and champain countrey and much suspected, it is good to place Sentinells 200 or 300 paces from the quarter, answering one upon another (as upon all occasions they must be) as in a circle round about it. And these not to stand near the wayes or principall approches, (as the manner is) but alwayes passing to and fro, one towards another, as if they would change places : By which continuall motions none may passe undiscovered. As farre beyond these, they which went to discover have their courses, sometimes riding up even to the adverse garrisons (if they be not too farre distant) which shall be shewed at large in the next chapter.

CHAP. VIII.

Of Scouts to discover the high-wayes.

THe quarters being thus accommodated, the Commissarie Generall shall depute a Corporall with 12 or 15 horse, and a trumpet to discover or scoure the high-wayes towards the enemies abode; without which diligence the enemie might charge the Sentinells so suddenly, and enter with them, as there would be no time for the Corps-du-guard and others to prepare themselves for defence. These do consist partly of Cuirassiers, and partly of Harquebusiers, to give the alarm. They are to advance towards the enemie some three or foure houres march, by the severall highwayes, foure or five to a way, as occasion shall require. They must not set foot on ground, but must silently go, listning if they heare any rumour, which in the [a] night is easie to be heard. If they heare any thing without being discovered, the Corporall shall secretly send word to the quarter by a souldier of the approch of the enemie. And when he judgeth the first is arrived, he may send a second to assure the former advice; retreating by little and little, and observing the enemie and the number of his horse : which he may easilier guesse by their footing, then by view. But if the enemie perceived him, he shall cause a carabine or two to be discharged, and shall speedily dispatch away a souldier to certifie the quarter. Or if the enemies number be great, he shall set on fire some house thereabout, they of the quarter knowing beforehand wherefore it is done. And sending two souldiers with more certain news, they shall give fire to their carabines when they be so near the quarter as that they may be heard, thereby to give them the more time to get ready. If the quarter be in a very suspicious place, more companies of discoverers must be sent out: and they are to have a countersigne given them (as the name of some town, &c.) to know each other by in the night.

a *Tutius operiantur exploratores nocturnis quàm diurnis, in quodammodo ipse sui proditur inventor, cujus speculatores fuerit ab adversario deprehensi.* Veg. lib. 3. cap. 6.

Alarms

Alarms (though false) cannot be prevented, it being in the enemies choice to shew himself as often as he please; happily for no other intent but to wearie your souldiers ; or by that stratagem to make them secure and carelesse. To remedie this , the Captains use to give the alarm secretly (without sound or noise) by silent advices; that so the enemie vaunt not of putting you to trouble, but wearie himself. And thus the horrour of the sounds of trumpets and noise of warlike cries is avoided , which hinder the hearing of the Commanders directions. But if the enemie charge the said Discoverers or Sentinells so hard, as that they have no opportunitie to send word, but the enemie puts on to enter the quarter with them (which is the best way for him to compasse his purpose) then they shall (flying to the quarter) give the alarm with firings of the Harquebusiers and calling out aloud, entering not at the usuall wayes, but at the private ones; to give the enemie occasion of suspence, not knowing whither they might draw him on. Moreover, when the alarm is thus secretly given (as before shewed) and having some notice of the enemies forces how strong they are in number , you may cause your souldiers to mount with all possible secrecie, and order them for fight, on the flank of the enemies advenue, leaving the Sentinels (with some trumpets) there standing, with command that, when the enemie approcheth them, they shall [b] bravely sound an alarm. Whereupon the enemie (if he be a souldier) will charge them in full career with one squadron to enter with them, and then second those with the rest of his troops: whereupon it will be hard (especially in the night) to keep the souldiers from pillaging. The first (entring without resistance) will be scattered about the houses; the rest will hasten to get their shares : and whatsoever the Captains do , they shall not be able to keep them in such order as they ought. Then shall your troops resolutely charge them, not doubting of a good issue , they being now surprised which thought to find you asleep. Or if it be not thought fit to fight, yet may you by this means make a safe retreat, so as you be not troubled with too much baggage,

If there be no bridges or strait passages between the quarter and the enemie, by which he must necessarily passe, the further the discoverers ride towards the enemie, the better; if he lay in garrison (so as the distance be not too great) they may ride to the very gates. But if there be such strait passages or bridges by which the enemie must of necessitie passe if he will assail the quarter, there must be guards of Harquebusiers placed, which by their giving fire, or otherwise , shall give notice if the enemie shall approch. Sometime a whole companie is to be sent out upon this service, being a guard for the whole armie,

Spanish manner is when they go to charge) but could neither see nor be seen by reason of the winding of the way in the wood. Upon this he commanded the Drums and Trumpets to stand, and found a charge : whereat the enemie made a stand , expecting to be charged; which gave time for all the troops to get into the plain, by hastening their march. *Manuscripts penned by Sir Fran. Vere, of his own exploits, &c.*

b Such a stratagem was used by Sir Fran. Vere, Anno 1589. who being to passe through a wood near Lier, the enemie from that castle came forth, to gall them in their passage. Sir Fran. with 50 horse and 6 trumpets made a stand about the middle of the wood, halting the troops and carriages out of the wood into the plain, placing too sone with 6 Drums in the rear. The enemie gave 3 shouts (as the

CHAP. IX.

Of forraging.

FOrraging is an action of great importance and danger. 1. Of importance, because thereon dependeth the sustenance of the horses. 2. Of danger, by reason of [a] the enemies endeavours to set upon the guards and convoyes of forragers, which must be sent out at least twice a week. Therefore, that these forragers may the better be secured, there must alwayes be a good grosse of Infanterie and Cavallrie sent with them, under the command of a chief officer, or at least a well experienced Captain. The Provost or one of his assistants is to go with them, to punish such as are exorbitant or straggle. If the forrage be for the whole armie, the Lieutenant Generall is to leade the convoy. [b] The baggage nor horse-boyes must be mingled among the troops.

It is not fit to go twice together to one place to forrage, lest the enemie knowing it, watch an opportunitie. At first it is good to forrage in the most remote places, and where the enemie is like to come to encamp : but if the enemie be settled, it is not good to forrage so near him as that he might set upon the convoy with Infanterie and Cavallrie; but rather in such places, where he can hardly (without great danger to himself) endammage the forragers. [c] If there be one or more streets by which the enemie might come, between the quarter and the place of forrage, some convenient number of foot , and ten or twelve horse must be left at the advenues of each of the said streets. The horse are to place a Sentinell , and to send out two to discover the wayes a good distance before them. By this means the forragers having finished their forraging, make their retreat safely; to which purpose also one or two troops of twentie five horse apiece use to march upon the flanks of the forragers. When all the forragers are marching back again towards the quarter, all the convoy marcheth in the rear; it being unlikely that the enemie will set upon them with any great forces between their convoy and their quarter.

At the place of [d] forrage , the Chief shall cause a troop of Harquebusiers to advance somewhat before the rest, there to stand and to suffer none to passe beyond: he is also to send out some souldiers on every side, and to visit woods and valleys, &c.

For the better securing of the said forragers, or the quarter, there use to be fiftie or more of the Infanterie (which may be fitly performed by Dragoneers) with a competent number of horse, placed in some castle or strong Church within two or three houres riding of the quarter. But to se-

a Hostes qui longè à suis aut pabuli, aut præda gratiâ commorantur, subitò occupandi cum delectu. Veg. lib. 3. cap. 10.

b Pugnatores ab impedimentis laxamento aliquo dividuntur, ne constipati ladantur in pralio, ambulante exercitu. Ibid. cap. 6.

c Ut locorum varietas adveniret, in defensionis ratio varietur. Ibid.

d Ubi pabulandi tempus fuerit, alii pabulum colligant, alii apparatu instructique sequantur, ut ne si omnes se ad pabulum colligendum convertissent, & subito quadam irruptio aut insidia fierint, ipsi imperati sparsiq; opprimantur. Leo Tact. cap. 17.

ture the quarter, there ought to be two places equidistant so guarded, which might cut off those small troops which run near the armie on either side. And if the troops be of number, these may (by their discoverers or spies) receive notice thereof, and so suddenly inform the quarter.

CHAP. X.
Of Garrisons.

a *Adversus omnia profuit, militi quotidiano exercitii robore, &c.* &
b *Securi in desides vindicare.* Veg. lib. 1. cap. 1. *Exercitus labore proficit, otio consenescit.* ibid. lib. 3. cap. 26.

c Anno 1582. the town of Zutphen was taken and surprised by certain souldiers, which by night had conveyed themselves close to the gate; at the opening of which (in the morning) they violently rushed in, and kept it, till more supplie came. *Meteren.* lib. 11.
d *Vastatu, disposito per occultu milite, paucos misit qui abigerent pecora Segobrigensium, ad qua illi ondeme a, cum frequentes precurrissent, simulantesque fugam praedatores*

BY reason of the affinitie between a camp and a garrison, it will not be amisse (though somewhat by way of digression) to say something of them. The fittest places for the Cavallrie to be laid in garrison are those which are frontiers towards the enemie: thereby the enemies excursions are hindred, and their own friends secured. Whereas otherwise (though they be never so strong of Infanterie,) they are like to have some of the enemies horse alwayes at their gates. Besides, it gives more courage to the Cavallrie to have their garrison thus on the frontiers, against the time of their going out upon service, then if they had spent all the winter [b] lazily in some garrison more within the countrey. It is good to appoint them their ordinary settled garrisons, that so they may there leave their baggage, and go into the field with the lesse incumbrance; which will also make them the better skilled in the knowledge of the countrey and wayes. If there be one troop or more of horse laid in garrison in some walled citie where the horse make no guard, the Captain of each troop must alwayes keep one of his souldiers in the Corps-du-guard of the governour, to give him notice of all occurrences, of the enemies approches, alarms, &c.

Besides, it is fit that a troop of horse having a frontier citie for their garrison, should keep fifteen horse upon the guard; if there be more companie, then twentie five at least, to be presently readie upon all occasions, while the rest can prepare themselves. And alwayes at the opening of the gates, every morning, two or more horses are to be sent out to discover about whether there be any embuscadoes. For the securing of your discoverers some ordinance is alwayes kept ready, and untill they return none are to be suffered to go out of the gate.

If the countrey about the garrison be champain, happily the enemie lying near may have an embuscadoe two or three leagues off. And the better to draw you into it, he may send out some horse (the day before) within sight of your garrison; which returning the same way [d] (some driving cattel, others carrying sacks, &c.) may draw out some of your horse to regain their bootie, whereby you might fall into their embuscadoe. In such cases you must observe such cautelous diligences as shall be shewed in the [e] chapter of embuscadoes.

If those which you shall send out to discover meet with no boores, or that they come not to the garrison as they were wont, it is a signe they are stayed by the enemies embuscadoe.

If an alarm be given in the night, those souldiers which have the guard must presently mount; their Chief must instantly send two one way, and two another way to run about the ramparts of the place, to take notice and to report wherefore the alarm was given: if the rumour continue, the rest are to run thither with all expedition. But this diligence of keeping the horse at the Corps-du-guard is not of necessitie in such garrisons which lie within the countrey, where there is no fear of surprises, or scaladoes.

persequerentur, deducti in insidias, caesique sunt. Frontin. Strat. lib. 3. cap. 10.   e *Part.* 4. cap. 3. The like stratagems and embuscadoes have been practised in the late warres. Anno 1599, Count Lodowick of Nassau by the like device drew the Count Busquoy out of his garrison of Sevenaer upon an embuscadoe, where Busquoy himself was taken prisoner (among others) which cost him 20000 guilders ransome, and the town it self taken. *Meteren.* lib. 21. 433.

CHAP. XI.
Of Spies.

a *Nulla transilia meliora sunt, quàm illa, quae ignoraveris adversarius ante quam facias* Veg. lib. 3. cap. 26. *Metellus Pius, in Hispania interrogatus, Quid postridie facturus esset, Tunicam meam si id eloqui posset (inquit) comburerem.* Frontin. Stratag. lib. 1. cap. 1. *Veteres Minotauri*

THe best and principall means for a Commander to avoid divers inconveniences, and to effect many worthy designes, are, First, [a] to be sure to keep his own deliberations and resolutions secret, [b] Secondly, to penetrate the designes and intentions of the enemy. For which purpose it behoveth him to have good spies, which must be exceeding well rewarded, that so they may be the readier to expose themselves to all dangers. The best and most assured spies are ones own souldiers, which (feigning some discontent for want of pay, or otherwise) enter into the enemies service, and get themselves into the Cavalry, as having best opportunity (whether in the field or in garrison) to give information. Of these it is good to have many, and in severall places, the one knowing nothing of the other. You are to agree with them of the place where they shall convey their letters, as some tree, gallows, or other place easie to find, where they also shall find yours giving them order to come in person when their advice is of great importance: as, if the enemy would fall upon a quarter, surprise some place, or attempt some other great enterprise. There

signum in Legionibus habuerunt, ut quemadmodum ille in intimo & secretissimo labyrintho abditus prohiberetur, ita eorum consilium semper occultum esset. Veg. 3. 8.
b *Explorandum est si he us quid hostis molitatur, in praesenti, vel in futurum possimus agnoscere.* Veg. lib. 3. cap. 6.   Livius giveth Annibal this commendation, *Omnis ei hostium, haud secus quàm sua, nota erant.* lib. 21. For want of good intelligence, many inconveniences have befallen divers commanders. *Romy omnis* (as Livie reporteth) *having thought against the Equi all might passed them, thinking himself beaten, without further enquirie, made towards Rome:* the *Equi* also deeming themselves overthrown, withdrew their armie into their own countrey. The same might be paralleled by divers modern examples, for which I referre the reader to our modern historians.

might

might also divers souldiers be daily sent disguised, under severall pretences, to observe what is done in the enemies leaguer, when it is near. The boors use also to serve for spies, aswell women as men, which, being not much regarded nor suspected, may have the freer accesse : but these are not alwayes to be trusted, neither are they so well able to judge of or to pierce into businesse, and the lesse assurance and information is to be had by their relations.

There are also spies which are called double, which must be men of great fidelity. These (to get credit with the enemy) must sometimes give him true information of what passeth on the other side; but of such things, and at such times, as they may do no hurt. But these kind of spies cannot continue long without being discovered.

If it be possible, such spies must be had, as are entertained into domesticall service of the chief officers of the enemy, the better to know their intentions and designes.

On the other side, there must be exceeding great care taken to beware of the enemies spies, which otherwise may do you as much mischief as you reap benefit by your own. To remedy this inconvenience,

1. Those which shall be discovered must be punished with extreme rigour, which will be a means to deterre others which are or might be so imployed.

2. Rogues, vagabonds, and idle persons must be chased out of the leaguer.

3. No officer is to entertain any unknown person into his service. For oftentimes at table and otherwise things happen to be spoken, which were more fit to have been kept secret.

4. No stranger is to be lodged within the quarters by any officer or souldier without speciall license. To this purpose a sudden [c] command useth to be published, for every man to repair to his tent or cabin, whereby the Provost takes such as are remaining in the streets ; which are made to give account of their businesse there.

5. A means may be used to deceive the enemy by his own spies, giving it out that you intend one thing, and do a contrary: also by seeming no way mistrustfull of the enemies drummes and trumpets (which are often sent with some pretended message, to heare and observe) and letting fall some words (which carry with them some probability) in their hearing, which they may take for truth.

6. [d] Sometimes it is wisdome, having discovered a spie, in stead of punishing of him, to tell him that (out of a good Inclination to him) in stead of severe punishment, you desire to do him good, &c. by such baits they may become double spies. And if you suspect any of your own souldiers, it is best to dissemble it, and to make much of them, the better to discover them.

[e] Lastly, no drumme nor trumpet of the enemies is to be admitted into the leaguer, but first to be stayed by the Sentinells of the Cavallry, untill notice be given to the Lord Marshall, and he give leave for their admission: then they are to be committed to the provost Marshall, which suffereth no man to speak with them. The Lord Marshall having understood their message, acquainteth the Lord Generall therewith, that so a course may be taken for their dispatch. Other wayes and means may be used for discovering and preventing of spies, wherewith the ready [f] invention of a quick-spirited Commander will abundantly furnish him upon every occasion.

c *Cùm explorator hostium litteras oberrat in castris, omnes ad tentoria sus per diem redire jubentur, & statim deprehenditur explorator.* Veg.lib.3,c,26.
d *Si speculator hostium reperis, nè uno eodémque modo illos tractaveris, &c.* Leo Tact.cap.17.
e Edict for Marshall laws, Art. 13.
f *Soleria enim imperatoris, ubi occassionem rerum gerendarum capvit, non in iis solum quæ invenue sunt consistit, sed etiam multò plura ac sepe meliora excogitat,* Leo Tact.cap.18.

CHAP. XII.
Of dislodging.

FOr the manner of dislodging or removing of the Cavallry out of the quatter, there are also necessary advertisements to be given.

All the Cavallry lodging together, and order being given for their remove, the Commissary Generall is to take notice of the precise houre: and at the distributing of the word to the Quartermasters, he is to warn them to give notice thereof to their Captains; which must be carefull to cause the [b] boutez-selle to be sounded when they heare the Generalls trumpets do it. This useth to be sounded two houres before the time of departing, and the *A chevall* when it is time to march. Upon sudden occasions, or for privacy, no other warning is given but onely the [a] Generalls trumpets sound, and the rest take it from them.

If the Cavallry be quartered in severall places, the Quartermasters (coming for the word [c] the evening before) carry the orders to the Captains, acquainting them with the just houre for their assembling at the generall Rendez-vous. If the remove be sudden, word is carried by one of the two souldiers which attend the Generalls as is before shewed: In suspected places they are to remove with all possible silence.

The Rendez-vous where the troops must assemble, to be ready to march, must be out of the village, and free from hedges, &c. (though it be somewhat the further off) towards the place to which they are to march. The company which hath the vanguard is to be first on their march towards the Rendez-vous; the souldiers of every company assemble at their Cornets lodging, who is to be first on horse-back; and the [d] Captain by his readinesse is to give good example to his souldiers. The greater part of the company being met, the Captain is to advance towards the Rendez-vous.

a With antiquitie it was usuall to remove or dislodge, by sounding the trumpet three times. Leo c.17.
b *Induces unus insonuit, mox aliquatuer responderunt.* Diod.19.
c *Scipio tesseram vesperi per castra dedit, ut anti lucem viri equique curati & pransi essent, omnia s equus frænatos teneret eques.* T. Liv. lib.28.
d John, Duke of Calabria is said upon all occasions to have been le premier homme armé, & de toutes pieces, Phil. de Comines, lib.1. cap.12.

The

The company which that day hath the guard, muſt not ſtirre untill all be gone, their Lieutenant going to the contrary ſide of the village (remoteſt from the Rendez-vous) to draw in his Sentinells. All the troops and baggage being marched away, the ſaid company ſhall alſo march. But if the ſaid company be to march in the van or battaillon (to ſave the travell of the horſes to haſten to their place of march, and the trouble of paſſing before the other troops) it is beſt to commit that duty to the company of Harquebuſiers which is to march in the rear of all.

Every Lieutenant (when his company marcheth) is to ſtay to reprehend or *d* ſeverely puniſh ſuch as ſtay behind, eſpecially doing it to pillage, or for the like bad intent. The Provoſt or his aſſiſtants are alſo to ſtay to ſee the fires put out, and good order kept.

As the troops enter the Rendez-vous, the Quartermaſter Generall, or ſome of the particular Quartermaſters are to place them one after another in their due places, according to the written orders; leaving ſpaces for every company that is to come, which after two or three dayes they can obſerve of themſelves.

The companies entring the Rendez-vous muſt fit themſelves as for fight. The Captains muſt put on their caſques, ſo muſt the Cornets, &c. The Harquebuſiers muſt place their Carabines on their thighs. The Cuiraſſiers muſt hold their piſtols in their hands, the trumpets ſounding, untill all be come to their places. If they be there to make ſome ſtay, they may put off their caſques and alight a while, (with leave) but muſt not omit to place Sentinells on ſome high places.

d How ſevere the ancients were in puniſhing of aluſes, may be ſeen in that example of I nuilius the Centurion, who having broken a ſtaff about the bones of one of his ſouldiers, called for a ſecond, and a third after that, for which he was called Cedo aliaʒam, among the factious ſouldiers. Tacit. 1. Annal. Which ſeverity of theirs wrought ſo good effects (as *Frontine* reporteth) that the Romane army being to encamp where a tree laden with fruit grew within the quarter, it remained ſo laden and untouched when the army was diſlodged. *Front. lib. 4. cap. 3.*

The fourth Part.

Of Embattelling.

THE ARGUMENT.

OF all other military actions, the *a* chiefeſt is that of embattelling, or ordering an army for combat; which now (in the laſt place) I am to treat of.

The occaſions of combat for the Cavallry are many and frequent , (ſometime by a ſole company, ſometime by more troops, otherwhile by all the horſe together) of divers kinds, upon differing accidents, and thoſe (for the moſt part) ſudden and unexpected. Since therefore no *b* rules nor directions can be ſo full and ample as to meet with all ſorts of accidents, my purpoſe is to aim at the chiefeſt; and to ſhew,

1. How to aſſail a quarter; to give the charge in fight ; and to order embuſcadoes, by way of offence.

2. How to do, meeting with the enemy in marching; and how to receive the charge by way of defence.

3. How to order the troops in battell; firſt, by ſingle companies apart: ſecondly, by all the Cavallry united in a groſſe body.

*a Acies, ſi ſapienter diſponitur, plurimum juvat; ſi imperite, quamvis optimi bellatores ſint, malâ ordinatione franguntur. Veg. lib. 3. cap. 14.
b Nulla ars minus habet ſtabilia præcepta quàm militaris ars, adeò ſubita in bellis ingruunt pericula, & fortunæ varietas dominatur. Scipio Ammiratus, Diſſert. Politic. lib. 21. diſcourſ. 2.*

CHAP. I.

How to aſſail a quarter.

A Captain which is deſirous to gain honour by ſome enterpriſe upon the enemy, though much his ſuperiour in ſtrength, hath *a* no better way then to aſſail him in his quarter. To effect this, he muſt have good knowledge of the village and the countrey thereabout ; and if he can (by taking a little compaſſe) charge him on the rear or on the flanks: if there be any negligence in the quarter, it is like to be on thoſe parts.

If he cannot (by other means) get knowledge how their guards are kept, and other duties either obſerved or neglected; he may conjecture by the *b* qualities of their Chief, whether he be a good ſouldier or not; whether he be proud and haſty, or that he be adviſed and deliberate: for ignorance joyned with a naturall fury cauſeth a man to deſpiſe his enemy, and to think it a diſparagement to him (as an argument of fear) to uſe ſuch cautelous courſes in aſſuring his quarter; eſpecially knowing himſelf the ſtronger.

In the aſſailing of his quarter, there are two things to be obſerved ;

1. To make your approaches as near the village as poſſible may be.

2. *c* To hinder him from uniting his troops into a body.

Touching the firſt, the firſt troop ſhall advance (without any forerunners) as ſecretly as may be : and aſſoon as they perceive themſelves to be diſcovered (without loſing a moment of time)

*a In manſione dormientibus opportunum prælium ſemper inſertur, cùm hoſtis ut interimitur quàm præparare ſe poſſit. Veg. Ibid. cap. 29.
b Ad rem pertinet qualis ipſe adverſarius vel ejus comites ſint, noſſe, utrùm temerarii an cauti, audaces, an timidi ſcientes artem bellicam, an ex uſu temerè pugnantes, &c. Veg. lib. 3. cap. 9.
c In campis ſparſis, atque ſecuris, opportunum prælium inſertur, exceptis ſupertentibus vel breviſſionibus repentinis ex occaſione, quam nunquam dux exercitatus amiſit. Veg. l. 3. c. 19.*

ſhall

shall charge the Sentinells, and enter the quarter with them, and surprise the Corps-du-guard before they be able to mount on horse-back.

For the second, there must be an exquisite observance of the orders given, and not a man to disband. Suppose the enemy hath 1000. horse and you but 500, you may fitly divide your forces into five troops. The first having surprised the Corps-du-guard (as before mentioned) shall from thence passe to the market-place, with resolution to sustain any resistance which they shall meet with. The second troop (perceiving the quarter invested) shall follow upon the gallop closely united, and finding no resistance, shall possesse the alarm place, and send some horse to run through the streets, to keep the souldiers in; and to hinder them from mounting on horseback.

The third shall come fairly on to the said place, and so the fourth; which (leaving the third there firm) shall hasten to the place where they heare the most noise : then shall they alight and enter the houses, putting to the sword what enemies they find. The running of these horse through the streets, hindering the souldiers to mount, will surely make them think rather [d] of escaping by flight through the gardens or otherwise, then of resisting : neither can there (in such a tumult) be good orders given or observed. Therefore the fifth troop hearing the noise cease, may conjecture there is no need of their help to take the village; and so shall divide themselves into two parts, and inviron the quarter on the outside, to hinder the enemies flight on foot. The horse-boyes may fire a house or two, especially where the enemy shall endeavour to fortifie; then (as the souldiers) to enter the houses to pillage and take prisoners, &c.

d Nec insequentium ullum periculum est, cum vi'ti (quibus defendi poterant) arma converterint in fugam. Ibid. cap. 21.

Another way of assailing the quarter, is this : The enemies camp removing, the Chief or Captain must labour to inform himself of the place, where he purposeth to lodge that night ; and where the quarter for the Cavallry shall be : which may easily be learned, because overnight it is usually published : or having good knowledge of the countrey, he may conjecture it. He must consider the number of his enemies horse, and of his own, and though he be inferiour by half (as beforesaid) yet may his enterprise take good effect, if it be well carried. He must fit the time so [e] justly, as that he may come to the enemies quarter in the evening, before the guards be disposed, or the orders given. And if the distance were such, as that he must march when the enemy marcheth; he shall depart from his quarter with all secresie, and [f] pretend to march to some other place, taking a way contrary to that which leadeth to the place intended. And (when he thinketh fit) he shall face about, and march on the flank of the enemy as covertly as may be. But to do this, two things must be observed ; 1. That your march be through your friends countrey. 2. That you have more then one spie in the enemies Cavallry, so as they be not able to stirre without your knowledge. It must be also considered, that if you go to assail your enemies quarter, he may have means to discover your purpose by his scouts or otherwise, and so be prepared for you : therefore must you have a care to be provided for it, by taking good order beforehand, and securing your [g] retreat by placing a good number of Infantery or Dragoneers in the midway at some convenient place. Going about this exploit in the night (as the fittest and safest way) every souldier must have some token or signe of a [h] white colour on their casks, to distinguish each other by. It often falleth out, that the enemy (having got intelligence of some intention to set upon his quarter) keepeth extraordinary guards, and is very vigilant in the night; but in the day time they all go to rest and are carelesse, as fearing no danger : at which time many have been so found and defeated.

e Nam vel celeritas vel tarditas alicujus provenire quam constitutum est, propositum persepe nostrum intervertit. Leo Tact. cap 15. 42.

f A good commander (like a good wrastler) ought to make shew of one thing, and to put another in practise: to the end to deceive the enemy, and gain the victory. Ibid. cap. 20. Tutissimum namque in expeditionibus evidetur, facienda ab hostibus nesciri.

Veg. lib. 3. cap 6. *g Nam disciplina bellica, & exemplorum periti, nusquam majus periculum imminere testantur, quam in vicissit ab hostibus.* Veg. lib. 3. cap 21. *h* This kind of service is called a *Camisado,* because the souldiers use to put shirts over their arms to be distinguished by. So did the Duke of *Alva* his souldiers (*Anno* 1571.) in the night assail the Prince of *Orange* his quarter, *donnant une Camisade.* Petit. lib. 10.

CHAP. II.

Of giving the charge.

TO know rightly how to charge the enemy, is a matter of great consequence. If you meet the enemie marching in the day time, and he retreat, whereupon you resolve to charge him; you are first to send a troop of Harquebusiers to charge him on the rear, as followeth. The Lieutenant shall first give on with 25 horse charging the enemie upon a full trot or gallop : him shall the Captain follow with the rest of that troop. These are to be seconded by a company of Cuirassiers, as fittest to sustain the enemy, if he resist. But if the way be narrow, the said Cuirassiers shall follow immediately after the first 25 Harquebusiers, and then the Captain with the rest of them. The other troops shall second these, keeping alwayes a hundred paces distance between every company.

If you meet a troop of the enemies horse, your self having also but one troop, both of equall number, and that it so fall out that the enemy retreat; you are to send your Lieutenant with twenty horse to charge him in the rear, following him with fifty to the same effect, closed as firm as may be: the rest must follow at a good distance under a good Corporall, which shall not engage himself to fight (though the enemy turn head) unlesse he see his Captain and Lieutenant in great danger: and then he shall couragiously charge the enemy, to give time to those of his company to

reunite

a *Miles le-Riffimos habeat Dux pòst aciem in subfidiis præparatos: ut si enim hostia vehementiùs insiliut, nè rumpatur acies provident subitò & suppleant loca addiítíq, virtute, minimicorum audaciam frangunt. Hàc dispositione nulla melior invenitur.* Veg. lib.3.cap.17.

renuite themselves : a there being nothing more dangerous in combat, then to engage the whole troop at once; because if they never so little disorder themselves, they cannot reassemble unlesse they have fresh men to sustain the enemy. Besides, the mere sight of a reserve gives a terrour to the enemy, which (upon occasion) may charge him on the flank. And if there be but fifty horse in a troop, yet some ten or twelve would be left for a reserve. If the troop which retreateth be of sixty horse, at least fifteen must be sent with the Lieutenant to charge the enemy, so as he be constrained to entertain them, to give time to the rest that follow to arrive in grosse and united : for by your sending of a smaller number, they might save themselves without losse, by leaving onely some few to make the retreat.

CHAP. III.
Of embuscadoes.

a *Boni ducis, no 1 aperto marte (in q 10 est commune periculum) sed ex occulto semper attentant; ut (integris suis) quanto possunt hostes interimunt esse v-l terrentur.* Veg.lib.3. cap.9.

IT is an ordinary thing in warre, to study how to endamage an enemy, and to distract his forces: to which purpose all possible means must be used, especially when the camps lie near each other. The Cavallry must principally be employed to travell and molest the enemy, sometime by hindering him from his victuall, sometime by endamaging his forragers, sometime by sending some troops even up to his camp to take some booty, by that means a to draw him forth, and to make him fall upon some embuscadoe disposed beforehand in some fitting place.

To order your embuscadoes (or ambushes) as they ought, you must first know what number of Cavallry the enemy hath; if he have fewer horse then you, you may employ all yours, attempting to draw out all his, and to rout them. Or else you may employ some small number, by which you may (at severall times) make some good booty, the enemy not daring to issue out of his quarter. But if the enemy exceed you in horse, it is not convenient for you to make embuscadoes, unlesse it be with some few horse : for being a small number, you may easily retreat; but being a grosse, it might be entertained by part of the enemies Cavallry presently issuing, and those seconded by more, whereby you should be hardly able to retreat without disorder and losse.

b *Count Philip of Naffaw anno 1595. intending to set upon Mondragons forragers, w th 600 horse passed the river Lippe, to lay an embuscadoe. But being discovered by some of the enemies souldiers or betrayed (as Metern hath it, lib. 17.) was taken unawares and routed: himself and Comte Solms wounded to death, many others slain, and divers taken prisoners. The Romanes were exquisite in laying and discovering of ambushes.*
c *Qui superventus & insidias subsessas passus est, culpam suam non potest excusare: quia hæc venire potuit, & per speculatores idoneos ante cognoscere.* Veg.lib.3.cap.22
d *Deprehensa subsessa, si circumvenitur ab hoste plus periculi instinet quàm parabat aliena.* Ibid.c 6.
e *With antiquity embuscadoes were very frequent and were to be used by either party. Utriq; parti in itinere ad subsessas commonis occasio est. Nam qui præcedit, opportunas vallibus, vel*

b The good successe of an embuscadoe consisteth chiefly in their not being discovered, for which cause they are usually appointed to march in the night: or being to march a great way, to cause them to passe by those places in the night, where the enemy might most likely discover them. So proportioning the time, as that they might arrive at the place appointed for ambush before day, that so they may give time to lay their embuscadoe under favour of the night. The said troops arriving long before day, they are to be kept firm on the plain, and Sentinels are to be placed on every side. In the mean time you c must diligently search and discover about the place appointed for your embuscadoe, lest there should be any ambush of the enemies: then (being assured for that) you are to lay your embuscadoe before the dawning of the day, and to place Sentinels in places convenient, where they may be unseen: some on trees, others couched on the ground, to discover such places as they cannot descry from the trees. The embuscadoe must not be laid much before break of day, because (otherwise) they cannot discover the approch of the enemy, but at hand, and so the embuscadoe should have no time to come forth, and put themselves in order, and being so taken on the sudden, d they might be defeated in their own ambush. Besides, in that remainder of the night, many might be overcome with sleep, and not use that vigilance which is required. The troops must be placed at good distances one from another, that so they intermix not, nor hinder each other in time of fight. In making the embuscadoe with a grosse of Cavallry, some number of Infantery must be laid in ambush about the mid-way, to sustain the Cavallry in their retreat (if need were) or otherwise to assist them upon occasion. e In marching, some horse must be sent out a good way before, by the right way and the by-wayes, to discover whether there be no ambush of the enemies: And indeed, to be the better assured of the good successe of an ambush, it should be accompanied with some new and extraordinary invention.

If the Chief of a frontier garrison will attempt to endammage the enemy by an ambush, being inferiour in strength to the enemy, he must gather together so many of the troops of his neighbour garrisons, untill he be superiour. And by making embuscadoes two or three times in this manner, it will terrifie the enemy; in so much as that it may be conjectured, that though afterward he make embuscadoes with fewer horse, the enemy will not hazard to come forth, and so he may the safelier take booty. When the army marcheth, there is usually some Cavallry left behind in embuscadoe in some eminent place, from whence they may discover farre off, by that means to be secured from the enemies Cavallry, which usually is sent to charge the rear of the marching army, to take some prisoners, or to get intelligence. But these must not go to their place of ambush by the right way, but having passed the place, they must return to it by some by way, lest the enemy following them, discover them by their footing.

To employ all the Cavallry (supposed to be 4000, in fourty troops) in embuscadoe, three troops must be sent before towards the enemy, under an able Commander, giving notice onely to him

sylvassq montibus, quasi post se relinquit insidias, in quas cùm inciderit inimicus, recurrit ipse & adjuvat suos. Qui verò sequitur adversis seminis, longè antè destinat expeditos, ut præcedentem adversarium alcuus transitu, deceptúmque à fronte & à tergo concludat. Ibid. cap.22.

and the Captains where the embuscadoe shall be; and letting none of the souldiers know that any more horse are to follow them, lest any of them (in the enemies charge) being taken prisoner, should reveal it to the enemy. Of these three troops, one hundred are to be sent to the enemies camp, *viz.* fifty Cuirassiers with their Captain and Lieutenant, and fifty Harquebusiers with their Lieutenant. Of these Harquebusiers [f] 25 shall advance before with a good Corporall, attempting to take horses, prisoners, &c. as they shall be able. In view of these Harquebusiers, at the distance of a canon shot, 25 Cuirassiers must make *Alto*, under command of their Lieutenant, to receive those 25 Harquebusiers when they return with booty. The Captain, with the other 25 Cuirassiers and 25 Harquebusiers shall keep behind some half league off, divided into two troops; the Harquebubusiers being placed nearest the enemy in convenient manner, partly to succour the said fifty horse (which likely will be charged by the horse of the enemies guards) and also to make their retreat, wherein the Cuirassiers are of principall use. These foure troops must still retreat in fitting distance one from another, one of them still turning face to the enemie ; unlesse the enemy so charge them as they must be forced to flie in disorder. The other 200 horse (being 150 Cuirassiers, and 50 Harquebusiers) shall enter the embuscadoe, with their Chief, about half an houres riding off from the other fifty horse; which when they see returning and charged, they shall issue out: the fifty Harquebusiers first giving a charge rank after rank, then the Cuirassiers, leaving twenty horse in the rear to make the retreat.

The grosse (which had taken another way , lest the enemie should perceive by the footing that there was a greater number, and so should stay or turn back) must be in ambush about an houres march behind the said 200 horse. And seeing them return charged (as surely they will, the enemie thinking himself the stronger) shall suffer them to passe, and the enemie also, that so they may charge them on the rear when they see their time. For better assurance. it were good to lead out with them (as before was intimated) some [g] 500 musketiers, and 300 pikes, which must be in ambush about a league behind the grosse of Cavallrie, on the way by which the said 300 horse should return charged. These foot must take heed they be not discovered untill the enemie be come up to them , and then shall give them a full vollie to disorder them. Upon this, the grosse of Cavallrie (now issued out) shall charge them on the rear and flanks : and then the said 300 horse are to face about, and sustain the charge ; by all which means it is not like that the enemie can escape without much losse.

According to this proportion, a greater or smaller number may be ordered, so as, if you would make an embuscadoe with 100 horse onely, 50 of them must be sent before towards the enemies camp, or village where he is quartered. Of these fiftie, fifteen are to advance before the rest, to take some prisoners or horses : the other thirtiefive shall be in ambush about half a league behind them , in some place (if it be possible) whence they may see those fifteen : but if not, then to place two horse between themselves and those fifteen, to give notice when the said fifteen shall return charged. Whereupon twentiefive (of these thirtiefive) shall advance, leaving ten of the best mounted at the place, to let the enemie see there is a greater number of horse. These ten must make good the retreat, untill the other fiftie arrive which lay in ambush two leagues behind, with Sentinells to discover afarre off towards the other thirtiefive, between which (about the midway) two horse were also placed to discover the motions of the first fiftie, and thereof to inform these fiftie which were in ambush behind them. These, seeing the first fiftie return charged, shall let them passe, and then issue out against the enemie : the first fiftie (making their retreat by twelve or fifteen of their best mounted horse-men) having reunited themselves and taken breath, they must make [h] *Alto*, and assist the other , as hath been shewed. This order is to be observed when you have certain intelligence (by your discoverers) that the enemie hath no forces thereabout. But when you cannot be assured of that (lest the enemie with a troop of fiftie or sixtie horse, casually meeting with some of your said small divisions, should defeat them) there might be twentie or twentiefive horse first sent out , whereof fifteen to advance to take some bootie, the other staying about half a league behind in some covert place , shewing themselves when those fifteen return charged, so to give suspicion to the enemie, or to make their retreat. The rest might be in ambush altogether , some two leagues behind them , demeaning themselves as before hath been shewed.

In [i] grosse ambushes they must make their number seem as small as may be; [k] but in small ones, they are to make shew of a greater number then they have : for which reason, all the horse must not go out of the embuscadoe at once , but some twelve or fifteen (when their number is small) must remain at the further part of the wood, to favour the retreat of the rest, (as hath been said) and to cause the enemie to think that there is a greater number of them within the wood. To this purpose some six horse may be left some league behind the rest, a little out of the way; but so as they may discover if the rest return charged, and then shew themselves at the end of the wood (as before is shewed) to make the enemie think there is a grosse embuscadoe, leaving one horseman further within the wood then the rest, and he to give fire when the enemie may perceive or heare him, which the enemie may think was done by a mistake.

[f] *Pauci equites præmittuntur, validæ manus per alia mittuntur loca: primi ubi ad agmen inimicorum pervenium equites, tentant leviter, atque discedunt, &c. suis illi manu supervenient, opprimunt ignorantes. ibid.*

[g] *C. Cassius in Syria adversus Parthos ducens aciem, equitem ostendit à fronte, cùm à tergo peditum in confragoso loco occultasset: cum cederent equitatu, & per nota se recipiunt, in præparatas insidias perduxit exercitum Parthorum, & cecidit. Frontin. Stratagem.2.lib.cap.5.*

[h] The word *Alto,* or *Altre,* is used in all languages in Christendome, and signifieth to make a stand. I cannot guesse whence it should be derived, unlesse it should be from the highdutch word *halte,* which is (as we say) *hold,* and with us is used in the same signification.

[i] *Bil autem optimum instruendi artificium, ut plus infecas adversarii copiarum, quàm primo aspectu ostendas .Ælian. cap. 47.*

[k] *Sim paucum habeas exercitum, plures buccina sonent, ut magnam multitudinem hostium venire arbitrentur. Leo Tast. cap. 17. 28.*

CHAP. IV.

How to do, meeting the enemie marching.

a *Bonum Ducem convenit nosse magnam partem victoria, ipsum locum, in quo dimicandum est, possidere.* Veg. lib. 3 cap. 13.
b *In rebus asperis & tenui spe, fortissima quæq; consilia tutissima sunt.* Livius, lib. 25.
c *Observandum autem est, haud per iste, sine magna nec-essiate, ut pauca copie e'm migno & instincto exercitu dimicent.* Leo Tact. cap. 12. 36.

A Commander, marching with one or more troops, and chancing to meet the enemie, or otherwise having news of him, must presently resolve either to offer combat, or to retreat, or to attend the charge of the enemie: and herein he must govern himself according to the intelligence he hath, and the convenience of the [a] place. To get the more certain intelligence, besides his scouts, he shall send out (a good distance before him) a Corporall with ten or twelve souldiers, who (pretending to be of the enemie, if the countrey be at the enemies devotion) shall discover and take information, &c.

If you meet the enemie near his own quarter, and farre from yours, you must resolve with a generous courage to go and [b] charge him, though inferiour in number; it being often seen that valiant resolutions are seconded with good luck. But being near to your own holds, and knowing the enemie to be much stronger then your self, it will be prudently done to [c] save your men by the nearest retreat: making your retreat in good order, and taking heed you spoil not your horses by too much haste, but suffer them now and then to gather breath, leaving a Lieutenant in the rear with some of the best mounted souldiers. The retreat shall be by the same way you went, so long as day continues; but night being come, you must take some other way (though the longer) to return to your garrison, or quarter. Thus you shall gain time by turning away from the enemie by the benefit of the night; causing the footing of your horses to be defaced at the place where you left the way; for it is to be supposed the enemie will follow you by the direct way. To deface or put out the footing of the horse, if the way be dustie, two souldiers are appointed to stay behind all the rest, which draw a great bough between them along the ground, and so put out the marks of the horses footing. Or if there be a great number of horse, and the way be broad, then foure souldiers with two boughs do it. But if the way be soft, the Chief commandeth five or six souldiers to alight, and with their hands and feet to deface the footings; and in such wayes the horse are commanded to march with doubled files, and closed, for a little space when they turn out of the usuall way, that so they may trample the lesse. Besides, you may avoid the danger of being traced by the horse footings (especially in the night) by turning out of the way at some house, or through some garden, breaking the hedge on the further side, and going into the way by wayes unthought of: by all which means you gain time, whilest the enemie is constrained to spend time in discovering of your footing, and taking information of the way that you took.

CHAP. V.

How to receive the charge.

IT hath been shewed how necessarie it is, that the Corporall which is sent out with the scouts or discoverers, be a very able souldier, to know what to do upon occasion of unexpected accidents. One or more troops of horse being on their march, with their discoverers before them, if they shall meet the enemie, and perceive him to be the stronger, the said Corporall shall presently send a souldier to certifie the grosse, that they may retreat: himself with his scouts also retreating, but by differing wayes. For suppose the enemie hath received tidings of his contrarie partie, it is likely that (having discovered the said scouts) he will follow them, perswading himself that they flie to their grosse: by which means the grosse shall have time to save themselves, while the enemie is pursuing the said Corporall and his fellows.

a *Quintus Sertorius pulsus acie à Quinto Metello pio, ne fugam quidem sibi tutam arbitratus, milites dispersos abire jussit, admonitos in quem locum vellet convenire.* Frontin. Strat. lib. 2. cap. 13.

When the enemie is much stronger, and the other partie have neither time nor convenience to put themselves into good order; the Chief shall call with a loud voice, and command every man to : save himself: whereupon the souldiers disband into many parts, so as the enemie cannot charge them all: and so (especially in the night) many may escape. But this course is dangerous, and must be commanded with great judgement: howsoever, in all retreats, some of the best mounted must be left behind under a good Commander, to make the retreat.

b *Prince Maurice, at the battel of Newport, sent the messenger (which brought him the news of Count Bucquoi's overthrow) away to*

If passing by or through some village or wood, the first discoverers descrie the enemie, not being able to discern of what number he is, one of them shall presently come and certifie the Corporall which followeth with the other scouts, whereof the Corporall instantly certifieth the Chief of the troops; who thereupon puts his men in order, causing them to put their casks on their heads, (which otherwise in march they carrie at their saddle, or hanging on their left arm) and in some convenient place he maketh *Alto*, and resolveth according to the more certain news which the Corporall shall send him. Which since it may be such as may [b] discourage the souldiers, the Chief perceiving him coming that brings it, advanceth towards him, with one or two of his discreetest souldiers, and receiveth his message in private. Having heard his relation, he must presently resolve, either to retreat or to fight. If he resolve to fight (the enemie being so strong) he must give such orders as shall be fitting, especially commanding the troops to go serried close; and if

sea, and kept it from the knowledge of his souldiers: commanding away all the ships (to take away all hope of escape by flight) and caused his forces to march through the haven, to meet the enemie. *Metteren, lib. 22.*

there

where be divers troops, that they intermingle not, but observe good order : for it might so happen, that the enemie might charge him [e] so diforderly , as he might make head and endamage the enemie, especially if he have not one or more troops of reserve following him , well united and in good order:

e *Qui difperfis fuis, inconfulte infequitur; quam ipfe receperat, adverfario vult dare victoriam.* Veg. lib. 3. cap. 16.

CHAP. VI.

Of ordering the troops for combat, by single companies.

BEfore we come to shew the severall forms of battel which may be used among the Cavallrie, it will be fit to speak of their severall kinds of fighting, which they are to be practised in apart by themselves, before they be joyned with the grosse.

If a companie of Lances were to fight against foot, they were not to give their charge in an united bodie (neither upon this ; nor any occasion whatsoever) because even the second rank of them hardly doth any certain execution; but they were to charge them rank after rank, wheeling off to the rear; to that end keeping large distances between rank and rank. The same order they were to observe, if they fought against horse upon the offensive. For the defensive, the companie (consisting of 64, as before, *Part.* 1. *Chap.* 19.) might order themselves in this manner. Two ranks (of eight in rank) should face to the front: two to either flank, and two to the rear; leaving an open square space in the middle, they all standing back towards back, faced every way, to receive the charge wheresoever the enemie shall give on.

The same manner might be used in greater bodies , as should seem good to the skilfull Commander. If the Lances were to fight against Cuirassiers, [a] they were (by two ranks together) to fetch their careers , and so to charge them, especially on the flanks and rear : every second rank forbearing the shock, till the first had done it, and was wheeled off.

If one companie of Cuirassiers be to fight against another, your enemie charging you in full career, you are to make a [b] Carracoll, that is, you divide your bodie by the half ranks, and so suddenly open to the right and left ; so as the enemie passeth through you, and you (facing inward) charge him on the flanks, as is shewed in *Figure 6. Part. 4.* Or if two companies fight against two other, then they observe the same manner, but keeping each companie entire, as may be seen in the same figure.

It is also to be done by the Carracoll first, and then (the enemie being within you) to wheel to the right and left inward , and so to charge him on the rear, in full career. These forms (in *Walhausens* opinion) are of [c] speciall advantage, for the enemie (having charged you in full career while you went on upon the trot, onely on the sudden opening to the right and left) either (saith he) must run through and effect little or nothing, or (staying himself in the career) [d] disorder his troop, and loose the force of his charge : as by *Figure 7. Part. 4.* appeareth. The Harquebusiers must be exercised to give fire by ranks. The first rank, having given fire, is to wheel off to the left (unlesse the ground will not permit it, but that it must be to the right) making readie and falling into the rear; the second rank immediately gives fire upon the wheeling away of the first , and so the rest successively. *Walhausen* would have them also give fire by files, the outward file towards the enemie (whether right or left) advancing before the bodie, in full career, and so firing; the rest successively to do the same, and in this manner to fight against Infanterie that might charge them on the flanks. But others do utterly reject it, as too much exposed to inevitable danger. In their firing by ranks , the first rank advanceth some thirtie paces before the bodie, first on the gallop, then in career (as some direct) and so to give fire : the second doth the same, and so the rest. The Dragoniers being a kind of Infanterie, and doing their chief services on foot, (as hath been shewed *Part.* 1. *Chap.* 31.) it will be needlesse here to shew how they are to be exercised for skirmish; partly in regard there is no want of books for the [e] practising of the foot (though I dare say they exceed rather in number then in weight) and principally, because I desire to confine my self to that which properly belongeth to the Cavallrie. How they are to dispose of their horses in fight, hath been shewed *ibid. cap.* 31.

a *Par. 3. rangs de lances lui aller gaillardement donner par les flancs: car par ce moyen ils l'entr' ouuriront. Monsieur de la Noüe. Difc.* 18.
b So *Walhausen* would have it.
c So the said authour conceiveth; but it is very doubtfull. For by this opening to the right and left , you must turn croop, and then make a whole turn ágain , and so give advantage to your enemie. It were better therefore to cause three or foure files of each of your wings to advance on the sudden, and so to charge the adverse troop on either flank. And, to equall your enemies front, you might cause the half files of your bodie to double your front to the right and left by division. All which your troop must be acquainted with beforehand , and are to do it in a moment of themselves, with all possible dexterities.
d The principall strength of Cuirassiers consisteth in keeping themselves close serried together: for this the Germanes are commended. Il faut dire que les Allemans surpassent toutes les autres nations , parce qu'il ne semble pas seulement qu' ils soient serrez, ains qu' ils soient collez les uns auec les autres, De La Noüe: Discours 18. e So farre as concerneth the exercising of the foot in their postures and motions, I suppose Pr. Maurices his book, and Captain Binghams notes upon Ælian (with the appendix) sufficient alone : But I wish some bodie would go on, and fully handle that which belongeth to the Infanterie.

Fig: 6.
Cap: 6.
Par: 4.

Fig: 7.
Par: 4
Cap: 6.

CHAP. VII.

How the Cavallrie are to fight against foot.

A Commander having intelligence of some grosse of the enemies Infanterie, and resolving to set upon them, he must principally aim to encounter them in a place of advantage for the Cavallrie, that is, in an [a] open champain. He must also use all possible diligence to charge them, before they can be ordered for battel, though they exceed him much for number.

But if the said Infanterie be put in good order at his approch, (if the ground be champain, and the number equall) yet may they be charged by the horse : First by some troops of Harquebusiers (or rather Dragons, because they do execution at a larger distance) which shall give on on their front, flanks, and rear. These were to be seconded by the Lances (in small divisions) when they were in use; but now by the Cuirassiers, who shall make their benefit of such overtures or disorders as shall be caused by the said Dragons and Harquebusiers.

If the Infanterie exceed in number, and so be serried in a grosse bodie; it will be hard for the Cavallrie to rout them, as hath been found by experience by the Swisses, which still had the better of the horse, by the reason of their grosse bodies of pikes.

If the Infanterie be ordered into severall battaillons, the horse are to charge them where they perceive them most open and naked. But if the foot have possessed themselves of some place of advantage, as some wood, trench, or covert way, then the horse are not to charge them; though equall, or somewhat superiour to them in number, in respect of such advantage.

CHAP. VIII.

Of ordering the Cavallrie in battel.

THe forms of battel used among the horse (presupposing such as are made by election, in a free and spacious champain, and not such as are forced through discommoditie of place, or other respects) [a] are many; and do varie according to the ground and strength both of your own side and the enemies, accidents, and occasions. In all forms a principall care must be had, that the troops be drawn up from an even front, that so they may be free from disturbing each other in the retreat.

Basta reduceth these forms to foure sorts, and *Melzo* to three, (making the second and third to be as one and the same) which are these :

The first is, when the troops are ordered as in one file, every troop following each other in a single order : which form is utterly disallowed, because it bringeth but few hands to fight, and the disordering of the first troop must needs endanger all the rest.

The second is, when all the troops are placed as in [b] one rank, or one front; the one troop being placed on the flank of the other in a single order or straight line. Which form is also disapproved, because in it all the Cavallrie is engaged at once, the one not being able to succour the other, and having no troops of [c] reserve.

The third is, when the troops are ordered checquer-wise, in squadrous, enterchangeably placed one behind another : so as three or foure squadrons being in front, such distances are left between each, as others behind them may come up to the front, without hindering the former. [d] This form may well be allowed of, and is retained by the best Commanders in the present warres of Christendome : yet the forenamed authours have this exception to it, because the Harquebusiers having taken up the said distances would hinder the Lances then in use. And if they should be drawn from those intervalles, and placed on the wings, they must be exposed to the first assaults of the enemie.

The fourth kind of forms, they make the Lunarie, resembling a half moon : but in this they differ from each other in the manner. That which they call single, must needs be weak, their double form is better. But both these last forms (the Checquer, and the Lunarie form) shall be more fully represented in figure.

Walhausen maketh six sorts of battels: namely, 1. The Lunarie. 2. The checquer. 3. The Broad-fronted. 4. The Embowed. 5. The Sharp-pointed. 6. The Divided.

The Lunarie (as he makes it, and the figure, *Fig. 8. Part 4. cap. 8.* sheweth it) is good, and indeed better then that of *Basta*; but is improperly called the Lunarie form : for it is rather a Hollow, or Open-fronted wedge, like Ælians [e] *Coelembolos.*

His Checquer is as the forementioned; and allowable.

His Broad-fronted is also not to be rejected.

His Embowed (which by the name should be a Convex half moon, like [f] Ælians *Cyrte*) he maketh a meer wedge. The form is not so good, though the name be not so proper.

The Sharp-pointed (in regard there is but one troop in front, and that seconded but by two troops on the rear angles; then but one troop again, seconded as the first) seemeth not to be so

---

Marginal notes:

[a] *Si equitatu gaudemus, campos debemus optare; si pedite, loca deligere angusta, fossis, paludibus, vel arboribus impedita.* Veg. lib. 3 cap. 9.

[a] *Ordinandæ acium, solem & ventum ante prospicias.* Veg. lib. 3. cap. 14. *Una acies bellica forma non est, sed multa & diversa, pro varietate armorum, militum, hostium, locorum, temporum.* Leo Tact. c. 20 18? [b] *Si nimium fuerit acies attenuata, cito ab adversariis factâ impressione perrumpitur, & nullum postea potest esse remedium.* Veg. lib. 3. cap. 16. [c] The Grecians had their troops of reserve, and herein the Carthaginians imitated them, and these the Romans also followed. Veg. ibid. cap. 17. [d] *Exercitus contractus & quadratus, aut non in militum oblongus, ad omnium occessionem atque eventum firmus, utilis, atque tutus est.* Leo Tact. cap. 9. 34. The Grecians had three kinds of horse-battels; The Square, the Wedge, and the Rhombe (which is as the diamond battel.) The Square was held the best for the defensive, the other two for the offensive. Of these the Wedge is preferred, because it bringeth most hands to fight; the rear division of the Rhombe being of little use. Ælian. cap 18. [e] *De instruend. acieb.* cap. 36 [f] Which the Latine translation termeth *Acies incurvus;* Ælian. cap. 47.

d as the former, because it bringeth few hands to fight, and is very subject to be **g** overwinged
overfronted by the enemie, and so to be charged on the flanks.

The Divided, especially at so large a distance, I hold to be dangerous. True it is, that here
Dragons are used as foot, but whether so single and so extended an order be the best for them
e placed in, I referre to the judicious.

Now concerning these six kinds of battels, they are in deed and in effect but two : that is,
Cheequer and the Lunarie, as he calleth them; and from these grounds the rest be formed.

ut these forms being onely imaginarie, and withall wanting that perfection (in many
:ts) which is required in reall battels, I shall now (to give fuller satisfaction to such as are
rs of militarie knowledge) communicate some forms of embattelings, which never yet were
ished by any.

hese are true delineations of divers battels really ordered and performed by the absolutest
nmanders of our times, according to the exactest rules of art; and such as experience hath ap-
ed to be fittest for the modern warres.

or the better understanding whereof, I have thought fit first to put down these directions fol-
ng.

ll the forces of the whole armie (both horse and foot) are usually distinguished and divided
h three parts; namely, the Vanguard, Battel, and Rear. (as hath been shewed *Part* 2.
3.) Each of which parts is governed by its particular Officer or Chief; yet so as the abso-
command belongeth to the Generall. These distinctions are alwayes so understood, in the
of marching, to avoid disputes about precedencie; so as they which march formost are said
ve the Vanguard, they which march in the middle, the Battel, and they which come last
ar. And these divisions alter their names according to the place they march in, wherein
observe a diurnall change, as hath been shewed in the chapter above mentioned. But if we
take the meaning of these words (according to their proprietie and usuall acceptation) in
r of fight or battel, conceiving that that part of the armie which is called the Vanguard
give the first charge; and that which is called the Battel, shall give the second charge, and
earward, the last; it will prove a meer mistake. For we are to know that the first charge
be given by the first troop, or foremost orders of companies which are in front placed as
e rank, extended from the one front-angle of the whole armie, to the other : and so it were
sible for them to be commanded or directed by one Commander, or Chief of one particu-
uadron of the armie, by reason of the large extent thereof : for we see that the front of
rmie embattelled before *Dornick. Figure* 14. (which was farre inferiour to that of late,
yed at the siedge of the *Bossch*) took up **i** 6380 foot of ground (being in their close order
red for fight) which is above a mile and a quarter of our measure.

ides, if the Vanguard (as it is called) should give the first charge, the Battel (which then
second them) may chance to be of a nation not onely differing from the Vanguard, but at
ce with them, or else some grudge or disgust between the Chiefs. And in that respect they
either neglect or slacken the seconding or relieving of those of the Vanguard, and not use
ligence which is required. In consideration therefore of these and other inconveniences, it
that every squadron of the army be so ordered, as each of them may have their first, second,
ird troops; by which means every division shall both be commanded by their own Chiefs,
all also be seconded by those of their own squadron, or division, which will give them the
ourage and assurance. The manner therefore for the ordering of an army for battel, is as
eth; That squadron which is called the Battel, is placed in the middle, the Vanguard on
ht hand of it, and the Rear on the left: and all these (usually) in one front and single order;
giment (or sometimes one company, especially among the horse, as *Figure* 10.) flanking the
as in *Figure* 12.

m hence the first troop of every division is drawn up, and placed in an even front or straight
om one angle of the body to the other. At a convenient **k** distance behind these, the second
f every squadron is placed, in an even rank, as the former; but so as the **l** first troop (which
give the first charge) being to retreat, and this second troop to advance, they disturb not each
for which reason, convenient spaces are left in the first order or troop, for the second to
up into. The third troop is placed just behind the first, but at twice as large a **m** distance
e second, as the second is from the first; that so the first troop retreating behind the second,
ay have convenient room to make their retreat in good order. All this will appear in the
following, among the rest in *Figure* 9.

e Infantery and Cavalry be joyned together, the manner is to place half the horse on the
ank of the foot, and the other half on the left, as appeareth in *Figure* 12. 14. and 15. But
ccasion either of the enemy his ordering of horse within the body of foot, whereby he
annoy your Infantery; or for other respects of moment, some of the horse may be placed
the body of the army, as is shewed in *Figure* 16.

*d charge without disturbing each other. The third troop (Acies tertia) were the Triarii, which were placed behind the Principes, observing
ch intervalles as before mentioned. Vide Livium lib. 8. & Lipsium de milit. Rom. lib. 4. ubi etiam Aciei Iconismus.*   *m* 600 foot.

Marginal notes:

g Whereof Æ-
lian sheweth the
inconveniences,
cap. 50.

h So did the Ro-
mans; the Van-
guard they cal-
led *Cornu de-
xtrum*, the Bat-
tel *Acies medis*,
and the Rear
Cornu sinistrum;
as is shewed by
S.t Cl. *Edmonds,*
upon *Cæsars Com.
lib.* 1. *cap* 7. *Ob-
serv.* 1. out of
*Lipsius de milit.
Rom. lib.* 4. and
is handled at
large by *Leo the
Emperour, Tact.
cap.* 18.

i Six foot make
a fathom, 100
fathomes a fur-
long, seven fur-
longs and a half,
a mile. Five foot
make a pace,
1000 paces
make a mile.

k usually 300
foot.

l The Romanes
also ordered
their battels in
three divisions,
or troops: viz.
their *Hastati,
Principes,* and
Triarii. The first
were called *A-
cies prima,* and
these were the
Hastati which
were to give the
first charge, at
a distance be-
hind them were
the *Principes*
placed, wch
were called *A-
cies secunda:*
these were so
ordered with
spaces or inter-
valles, that the
Hastati (being
put to retreat)
might fall back
into these spa-
ces, and the
Principes might
advance to give

N.º 6

N.º 5

Figu: 8
Cap: 8
Par: 4

N.º 4

What distances be observable between Regiment and Regiment, between Squadron and Squadron, between each Troop, the second from the first, and the third from the second, the figures will sufficiently shew, and especially the scales of measure in every figure. For the more easie understanding of them, observe that every body of pikes is single hatched, thus and the muskettiers crosse-hatched, thus , the horse are left white or void, as in *Figure* 12. by which the other forms may be easily understood.

CHAP. IX.
Of certain ceremonies before fight.

HAving shewed by these former rules and examples, how the horse are to be ordered for fight, not onely by themselves, but also when they shall be joyned with foot: that which [a] now remaineth seemeth rather to require action then words. Indeed with antiquity, when the army was embattelled and ready for combat, it was usuall for the Generall to deliver some set sp^ech, either from some higher place of turf or stone, or at the head of the troops, and riding amongst the Maniples to encourage his souldiers. And they either with an acclamation, lifting up of their hands, or clashing of their arms, used to manifest their assenting resolution. Unto which kind of [b] allocutions the ancient Sages use to ascribe a marvellous efficacy, not onely amongst the Grecians or Romanes, but also those whom they then accounted barbarous, as the Britons, Gauls, Germanes, &c. as the histories of those times sufficiently testifie. Next to this, they founded the *Classicum* (that is) a generall charge; and this was seconded by a generall shout of the souldiers, or a concussion of their arms. Moreover, a [c] scarlet, red, or a carnation coloured coat or cassock was hung out upon the top of the Generalls tent: and a countersigne, or a word of distinction was given to the souldiers, as, [d] *Victoria, palma, virtus,* or the like, to know each other by. The Grecians used also to sing the *Pœan,* before the fight to *Mars,* and after battell to *Apollo,* &c.

Of all which ceremonies (which they duly observed, as found to be of very good use, and which were much graced by the solemne and stately manner of performing them) our times have retained very few. For as the actions of the modern warres consist chiefly in sieges, assaults, sallies, skirmishes, &c. and so afford but few set battels; so the practise of delivering publike speeches is almost grown out of use and esteem amongst our chief Commanders. Yet the late [e] Prince of Orange at the battell of *Newport* before the conflict, delivered a pithy short speech to his souldiers: adding to his publick Oratory, publike Orisons, and riding up and down, gave courage to his souldiers. The *Classicum* is still retained (that is,) to sound a generall charge, namely amongst those troops which are to give on. And sometimes the *Clamor militaris,* or shout of the souldiers, which was not onely an acclamation or assent unto the Generalls speech, but also a loud and dreadfull kind of noise which they used to make when they gave the charge, thereby to encourage one another, and to strike a terrour into the enemies: as the Turks cry, *Bre, Bre, Bre;* the Irish, *Pharro, Pharro;* the French, *Sa, Sa, Sa;* the Dutch, Wall aen, Wall aen, &c. But as for the countersigne or word of distinction, that is seldome used now adayes, unlesse upon occasion of some *Camisado,* or other exploits in the night, when the souldiers may easily misse those means to know each other by, which in the day time the light, the sight of the ensigne or cornet, their skarfs (required among the Cavallry) or long acquaintance, may afford them.

But these being but ceremonies (as I called them in the title of this chapter) I willingly withdraw my self from them. Neither should I have been desirous to have meddled with them at all, but that the example of others [g] (who have writ in this kind) led me unto it; and the respect unto my Reader (in common civility) required it at my hands; whom I could not well leave (after the sight of so many dumbe figures) without a word or two at the parting.

There remaineth onely now, that every one (according to his office, rank, and abilitie) strive for honour and victory; propounding to himself the goodnesse of the cause, and authority of the Prince, the command of the Leaders, the vertue of the souldiers, the honour of the conquest, and the disgrace and damage of the defeat. Above all, lifting up his eyes and heart unto Almighty God, from whose hands victory, and the means to obtain it, is especially to be expected. [h] *It is God that girdeth me with strength of warre, and maketh my way perfect. He teacheth my hands to fight, &c.* [i] *Blessed be the Lord my strength, which teacheth mine hands to warre, and my fingers to fight.* [k] *Through thee will we overthrow our enemies, and in thy name will we tread them under that rise up against us. For I will not trust in my bow, it is not my sword that shall help me. But it is thou that savest us from our enemies, and puttest them to confusion that hate us.* And to this purpose we may (not unfitly) apply that which *Hezekias* spake to his Captains and souldiers (by way of encouragement) after that he had fortified himself against the power of the *Assyrians,* [l] *Be strong and couragious, be not afraid nor dismaid for the King of Assyria, nor for all the multitude that is with him: for there be more with us then with him. With him is an arm of flesh, but with us is the Lord our God to help us, and to fight our battels.* Conformable to this was that admonition of *Alphonsus,* King of *Arragon* and *Sicily,* given to his sonne *Ferdinand,* when he sent him with an army in aid of the *Venetians* against the *Florentines,*

in

Margin notes:

a *Quid superest nisi pignus quâ jam minimum est, non verborum.* Lips. de milit. Rom lib 4.

b *Cæsars* army, being so dismaid through fear as they were almost brought to desperation, *(tantus subitò timor omnem exercitum occupavit, &c.)* was by a elegant oration of his suddenly revived. *Hac oratione habita, mirum in modum conversæ sunt omnium mentes, summíq; alacritas & cupiditas belli gerendi innata est.* Cæsar de bello Gal. lib.1.cap.9.

c *Tunica russa, punicea, vel coccinea.* Some resemblance hereof there is in the bloody flagge at sea.

d *Veg.lib.3.c.5.*

e *Meteren.lib.13.*

f *Petus. lib.15.*

† This by the Grecians was called ἀναλαγμὸς and by the Latines *Barri* at (the original of which words, is shewed by *Lips.* (*ubi supra*) yet afterwards when the Empire was become Christian, they used (when they were ready for conflict) to cry, *Νικητήριος τȣ σταυȣ,* δ, υ, that is, the victorie of the Crosse: as appeareth by *Leo* the Emperour (who reigned in the East from the year of our Lord 886. to 905.) Tact. cap. 12.69. *Cùm & conflictionum movet exercitus, consueta Christianis vox usurpanda est, usurpetur tȣ σταυȣ.* And after this, in the very charge they were to make their shout, as it followeth there 106. *Conflictionis tempore post vocem Victoriæ crucis, mignos atque altos clamores edere oportet.* Lips.de milit. Rom. Reusner. de arte stratagem.

h *Psal.*18 32.34

i *Psal.*144.1.

k *Psal.*44.5,6,7.

l *2.Chro.*32.7,8

in these words, [m] *Nunc maximè te admoneo, fili, nè tantùm aut tua, aut commilitonum audaciæ tribuas, ut putes absque Dei auxilio victoriam ullam haberi posse. Victoria (mihi crede) non hominum consilio & industriâ paratur; sed Dei Opt. Max. benignitate atque arbitrio. Scientia igitur rei militaris itâ demum profutura est, si Deum nobis pietate atque innocentiâ pacatum propitiúmq; habuerimus. Deum igitur inprimis cole, in eum confide, à quo tum victorias omnes & optima quæque provenire non dubium est. Quem si quando tibi iratum suspicaberis, cave contendas; imo quicquid ab eo tibi accidisse videbitur, bene consule, & patientiâ atque pœnitentiâ eum placa. Solet enim Deus, quos diligit, interdum malis afficere: & quos constantes in adversis videt, rursus in meliorem fortunam restituere.* And now for a conclusion (in stead of an *Omen*) I will adde that ejaculatory prayer of the Psalmist, [n] *The glorious majestie of the Lord our God be upon us: prosper thou the work of our hands upon us, O prosper thou our handy work.*

flor. lib. 3.

————— *nec me tua fervida terrent*
Dicta ferox: Di me terrent, & Jupiter hostis.   Turnus ad Æneam, apud Virg. Æneid. l. 12.

m Cited by *Reusnerus* out of *Panormit. lib 3. de rebus gestis Alphonsi.* and *Mariana lib. 11. rerum Hispanicarum. Omne robur corporum, omnis equilitas, armorúmq; apparatus, Deo non adjuvante, ab agmine formicarum prorsus nihil differt.* Niceph. Gregor. Byzantinæ Historiæ.

n Psal. 90. 17.

THus have I briefly (according to my weak ability) run through that part of the Art military, which principally concerneth the Cavalry : Which subject I have the rather chosen to treat of, because it is so little and so sparingly handled by those that have given us directions for warre, and lesse observed in our ordinary practise, especially in the exercise of our trained troops here at home. Wherein yet I do not presume to have attained unto that maturity which is required for the perfect knowledge and instruction of it; much lesse do I take upon my self to teach others (as I doubt not but there are many thousands that are a great deal better able then my self) but onely in hope that these my collections may serve either as a manuduction to those, that are desirous to be instructed in the first rudiments or confused knowledge of this Art: or else as an occasion to the judicious Masters of it, friendly and favourably to correct or supply what they shall find here to be amisse, or wanting. For my self, I shall account it a sufficient reward of my poore endeavours, if by my untunable jangling I may chance to toll and call in better ringers. But it is too late now (and at all times least of all expected in this kind of subject) to labour for apologies, or with Rhetoricall colours to varnish or dawb over the wants and imperfections of this discourse. [b] *If I have done well, and as the matter required, it is that which I desired : but if slenderly and meanly, it is that which I could attain unto.*

a Witnesse those frequent and sharp reprehensions, expressed in his Majesties letters, from time to time: among others, that of the 21. of September 1628 from Windsor; and the continuall and serious callings upon for reformation, by the letters from the Lords of his Majesties most honourable Privie Counsell, and the right honourable the Lords Lieutenants of every County.
b 2. Macc. 15. 38

FINIS.

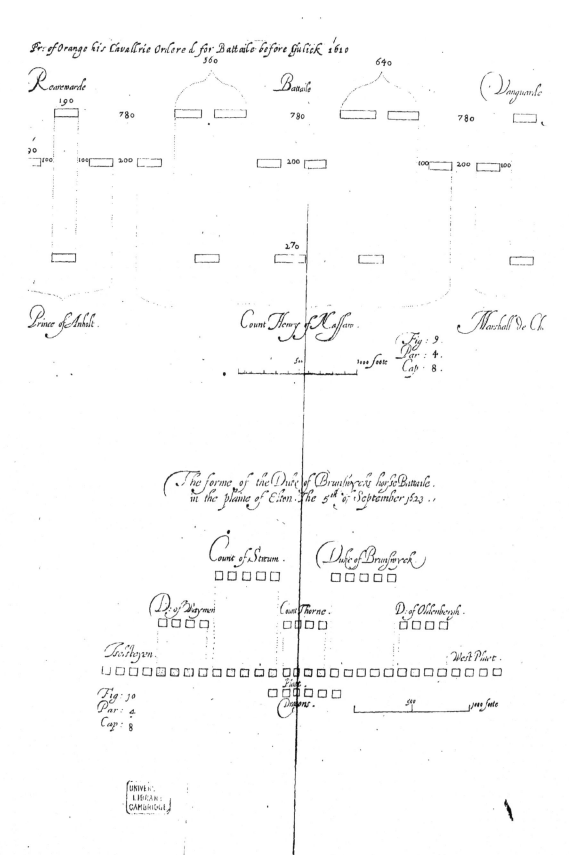

Pr: of Orange his Cavallrie Ordered for Battaile before Gulick 1610

560

640

Reavewarde

Battaile

Vanguarde

190

780

780

780

90

100   100   200   200   200   100   200   100

270

Prince of Anholt.

Count Henry of Nassaw.

Marshall de Ch.

500   1000 foote

Fig : 9
Par : 4
Cap : 8

The forme of the Duke of Brunswicks horse Battaile
in the plaine of Elton The 5th of September 1523.

Count of Strum.

Duke of Brunswyck

D: of Waymen

Count Thorne.

D: of Oldenburgh.

Tsorstewn

West Phart.

Fig : 10
Par : 4
Cap : 8

Pitue
Dragons.

500   1000 foote

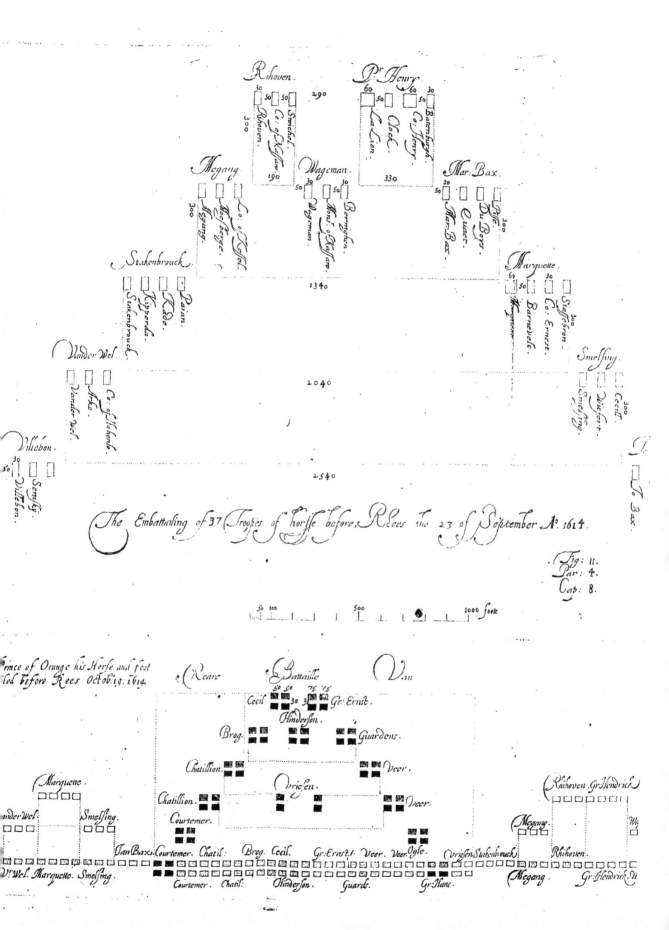

The Embattaling of 37 Troopes of horsse before Rees the 23 of September A⁰ 1614.

Prince of Orange his Horse and foot led before Rees Octob:19. 1614

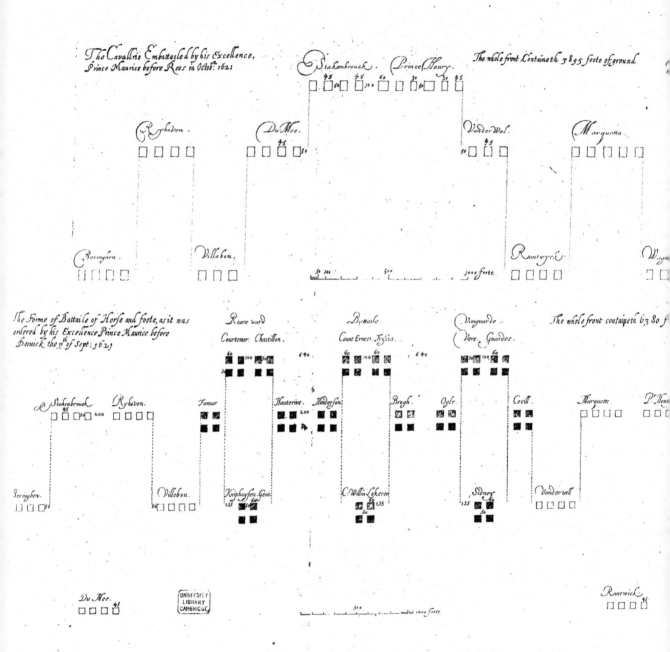

The Cavallrie Embattailed by his Excellence, Prince Maurice before Rees in Octob: 1621

Stakenbrouck. Prince Henry.

The whole front Containeth 3895 foote of ground

Rhodon.

Du Mee.

Vander Wel.

Marquette

Beringhen.

Villebon.

Rantwyck.

Wing

The Forme of Battaile of Horse and foote, as it was ordered by his Excellence Prince Maurice before Bomick the 1th of Sept: 1621

Reare ward
Courtemer. Chastillon.

Battaile
Count Ernest. Frilens.

Vanguarde.
Vere. Guardes.

The whole front containeth 6380 f

Stakenbrouck. Ryheven.

Famur

Hauterive. Anderson. Brogh. Ogle.

Cecill

Marquette

Pr. Nen

Beringhen.

Villebon.

Kniphurfen. Gent.

C. Willm Lokeren.

Sidney

Vanderwell.

Du Mee.

Rantwick.

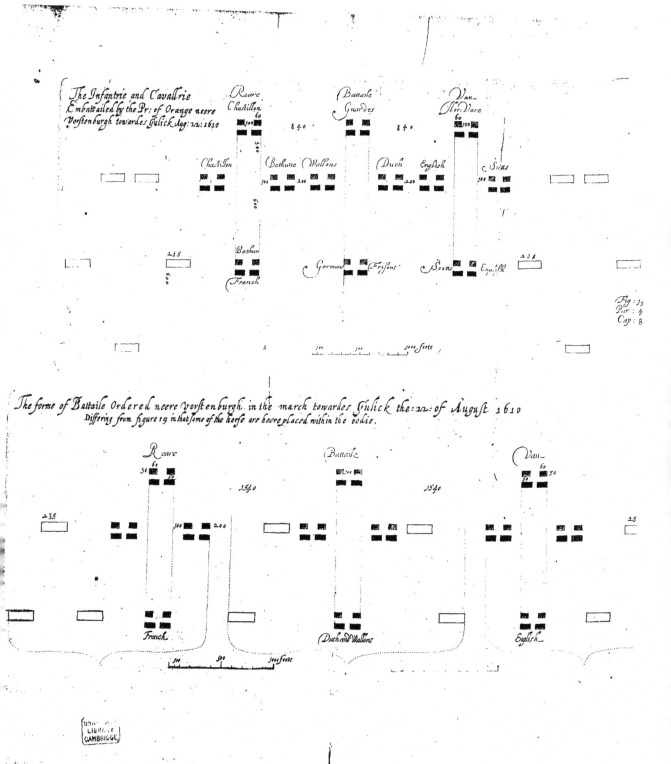

The Infantrie and Cavallrie
Embattailed by the Pr: of Orange neere
Vorstenburgh towardes Gulick Aug: 22: 1610

Reare
Chastillon
60
100
500

840

Battaile
Guardes

840

Van-
Her: Vere
60
100

Chastillon

Bethune   Wallons
100   200

Duch   English
200

Scots
100

600

Bethun

German   Frisons

Scots   Eng: IR

235
600

French

235

235

Fig: 15
Par: 4
Cap: 8

100   500   1000 foote

The forme of Battaile Ordered neere Vorstenburgh in the march towardes Gulick the: 22: of August 1610
Differing from figure 15 in that some of the horse are heere placed within the bodie.

Reare
30   60   50

1540

Battaile
100

1540

Van-
60   30
50   30

235

100   200

50

23

French

Duch and Wallons

English

100   500   1000 foote

Lightning Source UK Ltd.
Milton Keynes UK
UKOW04f2035080617

303015UK00010B/426/P